MW00345258

LANGUAGE AN
Dorothy S. Stri
Celia Genishi and Don
ADVISORY BOARD: Richard Allington, Kathryn Au
Carole Edelsky, Shirley Brice Heath, ᴜ

(continued)

For volumes in the NCRLL Collection (edited by JoBeth Allen and Donna E. Alvermann) and the Practitioners Bookshelf Series (edited by Celia Genishi and Donna E. Alvermann), as well as a complete list of titles in this series, please visit www.tcpress.com.

The One-on-One Reading and Writing Conference

Working with Students on Complex Texts

Jennifer Berne
Sophie C. Degener

Foreword by Douglas Fisher

Teachers College
Columbia University
New York and London

Published by Teachers College Press, 1234 Amsterdam Avenue, New York, NY 10027

Library of Congress Cataloging-in-Publication Data

Berne, Jennifer (Jennifer Irene)
  The one-on-one reading and writing conference : working with students on complex texts / Jennifer Berne, Sophie C. Degener.
    pages cm.—(Language and literacy series)
    Includes bibliographical references and index.
    ISBN 978-0-8077-5622-5 (pbk.) — ISBN 978-0-8077-7354-3 (ebook)
    1. Language arts. 2. Individualized instruction. 3. Education—Standards—United States. I. Degener, Sophie. II. Title.
    LB1575.8.B475 2015
    372.6—dc23

                                                                2014032563

ISBN 978–0–8077–5622-5 (paperback)
ISBN 978–0–8077–7354-3 (ebook)

Printed on acid-free paper

Manufactured in the United States of America

22   21   20   19   18   17   16   15   8   7   6   5   4   3   2   1

Contents

Foreword

According to motivational speaker Denis Waitley, "Failure should be our teacher, not our undertaker. Failure is delay, not defeat. It is a temporary detour, not a dead end. Failure is something we can avoid only by saying nothing, doing nothing, and being nothing."

I agree. All of us, teachers and students alike, should embrace failures and learn from them. I know it sounds strange, but failure should be an expected and honored part of every classroom. But too often, it's not. Instead, well-meaning teachers scaffold up the wazoo to ensure that students never struggle. Sometimes that means that students are told what to think about a text. I admit that I have told students so much about a given text that there really was no need for them to read it. Other times it means that they're excused from reading complex texts. And I'll admit to making decisions in the past that lowered reading expectations for students. I just wasn't used to having students struggle, and possibly fail. I only wanted the best for them and I thought that meant that failure was never an option. It is and should be.

That's not to say that students should only experience failure. Can you imagine what school would be like if every time you turned around you failed at something? Awful! There should be opportunities for students to experience success in a much greater proportion than failures. It's just that we have to accept failure, grappling, and struggle for real learning to occur.

One of the ways we can provide students with opportunities to learn from their struggle involves text selection. There should be a wide range of texts that students interact with on a given day. Some of these texts should be comfortable, designed to build readers' stamina. And some of these texts should be much more complex, challenging, and rigorous. These texts are selected to build readers' strength. It's a careful balance of strength and stamina that creates lifelong, skilled readers. One without the other is not likely to ensure that students can read increasingly sophisticated texts, or that they want to and actually do read texts. In other words, the stamina and strength work we do with students should ensure that they read more and better every week.

This sounds simple, but it's not. Providing students access to complex texts, without telling them what to think, is hard work. That brings me to the second thing we need to consider if students are going to access complex texts: scaffolding our instruction whether that be during whole-class, small-group, and individual interactions. We have to develop repertoires to engage students without spoiling the ending.

In other words, teachers need a range of prompts, cues, and questions designed to guide students' thinking without resorting to direct explanations. I learned this from a 4th-grader, Tino, who was meeting with me and a group of his peers. His group was reading *Hatchet* (Paulsen, 1987). He said, "Fisher, this time don't tell us why Brian does things. Just ask us questions to give us hints." Yes, Tino really said this to me. I had failed him and his group. But I learned from it. I learned to ask better questions and to provide students with prompts and cues to get them to do the cognitive heavy lifting.

The third thing we can do to support students' access to complex text I learned from this book. We have to engage students in meaningful conferences about their reading and writing. Interactions matter. They change people. In this book, Jennifer Berne and Sophie Degener provide readers with a road map for engaging students in conversations, conferences, that will change their understanding. They offer compelling case studies and a continuum that analyzes students' skills such that instruction can be appropriately aligned. Frankly, it's an amazing resource and one that has changed my thinking about classroom instructional time. I have been having much better conferences with students about their literacy development, especially as the texts have increased in their complexity, as a result of having read this book. I hope you find the information as compelling as I did and that you immediately begin to interact with students as they fail forward and learn at higher levels.

Douglas Fisher

REFERENCES

Paulsen, G. (1987). *Hatchet.* New York, NY: Bradbury Press.

Waitley, D. (2006) Retrieved from http://www.goodreads.com/author/quotes/5108.Denis_Waitley

Acknowledgments

We are grateful for the opportunity to write books for teachers, as this very important audience is always one that pushes our own thinking further than we might have imagined. In the catalogue of thank-yous, we are most indebted to the hundreds of teachers who have opened their classrooms to us as we tried out, adjusted, and revised our thinking (and as we continue to do so).

We wish to acknowledge the tremendous reviewers who helped us so much in the early stages of this book. Their thoughtful feedback was often the thing that pushed us to drop an idea to which we were needlessly clinging, to continue to clarify when we didn't think we could possibly add more detail, and to acknowledge our weaknesses and attend to them. Teachers College Press was exceptionally supportive in the process of sharing and annotating the reviews with their own perspectives. Our special thanks to Emily Spangler, who clung to the integrity of our ideas and understood which ones should be left alone.

Thanks also to Ivy Sitkoski, who brought a fresh pair of eyes to this project in our final stages of editing.

Our past and present colleagues have always been on our side. Though at this point in our careers they are too numerous to mention, we take special notice of Donna Ogle and Camille Blachowicz, who continue to act as our role models for, among many other things, intellectual generosity.

We would like to acknowledge The Shaw Fund for Literacy for its generous support of this project.

Our children serve as constant reminders that no two learners (even from the same family) are ever the same. We understand that we send them to school each day as one of many, but we hope that models like ours help teachers to make space for their individuality as readers, writers, and thinkers.

CHAPTER 1

Introduction

We have been greatly privileged by the invitations we have received to work with teachers in their classrooms. Although every context is unique, we have noted time and again how effective teachers can be when they work individually with students on their reading and writing. We have also noted how skillful those teachers who enact this kind of instruction are. We wrote this book to translate what we saw exemplary teachers doing into practical and concrete practices. We also wrote it to help teachers navigate the Common Core State Standards (CCSS) for English Language Arts, which have much potential to elevate our expectations for students in our classes, but also much potential for misinterpretation and confusion.

This book is predicated on the notion that teachers understand the importance of working with their students individually or in small groups during guided reading and writing workshop, even if their enactment of these practices is not yet to their satisfaction. We know that in order to justify the time demands of small-group and individualized instruction, the resulting learning must be robust. This is not the kind of teaching that can be thrown in casually as time permits. First, time rarely permits unless teachers make intentional space. Second, students need to be carefully prepared in order to manage themselves while the teacher is occupied with just one or a very few students. Although we have long committed ourselves to the idea that small-group reading instruction (e.g., guided reading) and individual writing conferences (during writing workshop) are essential components of students' literacy growth, we know that they must be meaningful interactions. Our work of late has been to study the practice of those teachers who work successfully with these methods in order to best determine how to assist those just beginning, or those uncertain about the effect of their current practice.

After observing hundreds of small-group reading and individual writing conferences, we have noted clear trends about the content of these one-on-one interactions. In writing conferences, teachers have typically focused on making tangible adjustments to the pieces students bring to the conference. During guided reading interactions, the focus tends to be on helping students to decode or make sense of the text they are reading in that moment. Teachers who approach individualized instruction in this way tend to help students come to a correct answer by coaching them to reread, to figure out a word, to add detail to their writing, or to identify and correct sentence boundary errors. We worry that such interactions do not necessarily transfer beyond the context of these one-on-one encounters. In other words, while a student during a writing conference might be able to add descriptive details about his dog in this particular piece, will he have a better sense of why and when he should use descriptive language in future writing? Will a student who is directed by his teacher to look at the caption under a picture in order to clear up a comprehension misunderstanding utilize the same strategy when reading independently?

During our classroom observations, we have also noted another kind of interaction between teachers and students, characterized by the notion that students need to "try out" reading and writing strategies in order to increase their facility with them. These teachers focused much less on reading or writing the text at hand and much more, it seems, on the strategy they were introducing or modeling to work on the reading or writing of the text. We refer to these interactions as stretch conferences because they seemed focused upon future tasks, and also because the discussions were not centered upon a simple solution to a reading or writing difficulty (i.e., use the glossary or add dialogue to the scene), but rather on the whole notion of how one reads and writes, a kind of a cognitive stretch. These seemed to be very different kinds of interactions, and we have spent much time examining them. This book makes an argument for the purpose of stretch conferences, deconstructs them, embeds them in practical classroom concerns, and helps teachers begin implementation. In this chapter, we introduce you to the theoretical and research base that underlies stretch conferences.

SHIFTING OUR THINKING ABOUT LITERACY INSTRUCTION

For many years, we have worked with teachers on bringing balance to their grouping practices. Though whole-group work is an important part of language arts instruction via shared reading lessons on comprehension, or vocabulary, or writing minilessons, we also know that students enter upper elementary and middle grades at very different levels, and teachers must differentiate instruction to attend to all students' needs. Like Ivey and Baker (2004), we see the individual interactions that teachers have with their students as critical to better understanding each student's reading and writing strengths and needs, as well as providing on-the-spot support to help them develop as readers and writers. We have found that teachers are very capable of adjusting their grouping practices (from mainly whole-group to whole-group and small-group and individualized interaction), but struggle to fulfill the potential of these interactions. Because initiatives like Response to Intervention (RTI) and the Common Core State Standards have influenced literacy instruction, focusing both on individual needs (RTI) and more rigorous outcomes (CCSS), teachers clearly need guidance regarding how best to capitalize on the one-on-one time they spend with students. We want these conversations to serve as scaffolds for students once they leave the conference and attend to a variety of reading and writing tasks on their own. This will increase students' capacity to read and write in more complex ways, even when their teachers are not there to support them. This book presents an alternative model for reading and writing conferences, one that is reliant not only upon the individual needs of a student at a given time but also on the absolute need to elevate our curricular demands, given new standards and literacy challenges.

Four theoretical ideas have helped us to create our model for attending to the demands of complex reading and writing in all sorts of classrooms. We discuss them briefly below. They provide the frame for the remainder of the book as well as the conceptual basis for stretch conferences.

THEORETICAL UNDERPINNINGS

Approximation. The notion of approximation comes from Brian Cambourne's (1988) Conditions for Learning, and it speaks to the importance of giving students permission to take risks as they learn. Teachers need to provide a supportive classroom environment that values this risk-taking, and sees student mistakes as a learning process that leads to growth. In Lucy Calkins's terms (2003), approximation involves trying on the ways in which more proficient adults engage in a task. Students learn by approximating adult behavior, often clumsily at first, before ultimately taking on this behavior and, in the best of cases, transcending it.

Construction of a Reader and Writer. Teachers cannot very well help students read for deep comprehension or write in specific genres for specific audiences if they don't understand the processes they themselves employ when doing the same (Jacobs, 2002; Moje, 1996). Teachers must begin to understand their own reading and writing in order to better support their students' literacy. Linda Flower (1987) carefully studied the cognition involved in the literacy practices of proficient readers and writers in order to make those processes more transparent and easier to understand. Subsequently, teacher educators (e.g., Routman, 2002) have helped teachers to employ metacognition in order to reflect on their own reading and writing.

Zone of Proximal Development. Most teachers have heard of Vygotsky's (1978) notion of the Zone of Proximal Development (ZPD). In brief, this is the idea that children have two developmental levels. The first is their actual level of development, what they can achieve on their own without support. The second is the level of development at which they can achieve if provided with strong support (i.e., scaffolding) from a knowledgeable other. The ZPD is the space between children's actual level and their potential level. Heath (2012) saw Vygotsky's ideas in action as she examined the role that parents play in scaffolding children's understanding of the intricacies of language.

Researchers (Dorn & Jones, 2012; Fisher, Frey, & Lapp, 2011; Palincsar, 1984) have adapted Vygotsky's ideas to literacy instruction, acknowledging the importance of a knowledgeable other (the teacher) in guiding student understanding.

The Place of Conferences. Though teachers can technically work within students' ZPD during whole-class instruction, the research (e.g., Allington & Johnston, 2002; Bayraktar, 2013; Block & Pressley, 2002; Taylor, Pearson, Clark, & Walpole, 2000) suggests that they can do so more easily and effectively during small-group and individual interactions.

The research on writing is much more specific in naming student-teacher conferences as one of the keys to improving students' capabilities in writing as well as their sense of confidence and self-efficacy (e.g., Bell, 2002; Flynn & King, 1993; Harris, 1995; Young & Miller, 2004). There is much less reading research, however, that investigates the student-teacher reading conference specifically. Nonetheless, the research that does exist (e.g., Boreen, 1995; Brown, 2013) demonstrates that reading conferences can be an effective way to support students' deeper and more complex understanding of texts. In addition, although Ivey and Baker (2004) and Allington and Johnston (2002) don't specifically refer to reading conferences, their work demonstrates the importance of teachers supporting students' growth in reading through one-on-one interactions.

DEFINING READING AND WRITING CONFERENCES

Reading and writing conferences have been around for more than 2 decades (Anderson, O'Leary, Schuler, & Wright, 2002; Anderson, Wilkinson, & Mason, 1991; Black, 1998; Gill, 2000; Haneda, 2004; McCarthey, 1992; McIver & Wolf, 1998; Newkirk, 1995). Coming out of the process writing and whole language movements, these conferences provide structures for students to share something of their reading and writing, and allow their teachers, in turn, to gain insight into individual students' literacy practices. We have always supported these important interactions and spent time trumpeting the virtues of listening carefully to students. In addition, however, in the last several years we have asserted that these interactions also serve as crucially important instructional moments. Because the time available to teachers and students for working directly together is so limited and becomes even more so as class sizes in many districts increase in response to budget constraints, individual reading and writing conferences provide a prime opportunity for the kind of individualized instruction not possible in a whole-group setting. As mentioned above, while we have been very successful in encouraging teachers to work through the logistics of providing space for individual conferences, it has proved harder for teachers to provide feedback that aligns with contemporary models of reading and writing that see meaning-making and powerful communication as goals of literacy instruction.

THE NEED FOR STRETCH CONFERENCES

Some scholars have interpreted the CCSS as a mandate against differentiation as it currently exists in schools (e.g., guided reading groups using leveled texts that researchers like Shanahan [2012] believe are not challenging enough). Because students are expected to demonstrate proficiency on a number of reading and writing tasks appropriate for their grade level, some argue that all students should be given the same materials and expected to perform the same grade-level tasks. While we do not believe that this is the answer for many struggling students, we do embrace the embedded idea that students only improve with difficult tasks set before them. We believe that student learning comes from struggle, and that a one-on-one interaction is a safe haven within which students can productively challenge themselves. We offer the idea of a stretch conference as an instructional context in which the teacher identifies an area where a student can grow and sets into motion the concepts that

> ### COMMON CORE CONNECTION
>
> Text complexity is a topic that has garnered much interest as teachers and administrators work to understand it We appreciate Beers & Probst's (2012) interpretation of text complexity, which includes a look at quantitative and qualitative measures, but also highlights the importance of understanding the relationship between the book and the reader. This provides an interpretation that necessitates, in our opinion, teacher understanding of individual students and their instructional needs and motivations.

will eventually lead to greater student achievement. This means that these conferences may not provide immediate gratification; the students' success in them is defined not as a demonstration of understanding in the moment, but as the beginning of new conceptions of reading and writing.

Stretch conferences require both student and teacher to move out of their comfort zones: The student is asked to do something complicated that requires deep thinking and, sometimes, time. The teacher also has to stretch out of the expectation that something is successfully taught only if a student can demonstrate it directly and immediately. Both students and teachers, as well as parents and administrators, have to know that complex literacy knowledge does not come quickly or easily (e.g., Fisher et al., 2011).

RECONSIDERING THE WRITING CONFERENCE

Consider the following example from a conference between a 3rd-grade writer and her teacher. The 3rd-grader has just finished reading her second draft of a short argumentative paper. The teacher is responding, in this discussion, to the first paragraph (quoted in italics):

> *I should not have to go to bed at the same time as my 5 year old sister. My argument is that kids should have no bedtimes once they are more than 5. I will be fine by monitoring my self. I will list the reasons why.*

TEACHER: Thank you for sharing this. Isn't the word *fine* one of those words that we've talked about that are very generic? Do you think you could come up with a different word there that would be more vivid and interesting?

STUDENT: Maybe like *safe*? "I will be safe because I know I will go to sleep not like at midnight every night"?

TEACHER: Sounds good. Let's see if you can replace that word and maybe other words, too. Good work.

We agree that the language in the student's writing could be more specific. We also have looked at enough writing curricula to

> ### COMMON CORE
> ### CONNECTION
>
> Common Core Anchor Standards 4 and 10 specifically mention the importance of understanding audience when composing a piece of writing.

know that using vivid language is a typical 3rd-grade learning goal. With this feedback, the student may return to her desk and come up with a more interesting word for *fine,* as her teacher has recommended. This kind of directive is well intentioned, yet it is not instruction that will actually help the student much as a writer. This interaction doesn't ask the student to think like a writer, who comes to decisions about which words may need changing based upon her understanding of audience and purpose. Consider the notions of approximation and Zone of Proximal Development, as defined above. The feedback given by the teacher is so specific and, in fact, easy for the student to accomplish that she will likely complete it to the teacher's satisfaction in a matter of seconds. There is no need for the student to take a risk, to approximate. Similarly, one could argue that this kind of feedback doesn't push the student into her ZPD. Therefore, the conference is a missed opportunity. The student likely has little idea why the teacher chose the word she asked her to change, and she need not think that through. She will merely replace the word.

Through our classroom observations, we have learned that teachers tend to use conference time to ask students to work on something that they are sure they are capable of accomplishing on their own. Remembering the notions of approximation and Zone of Proximal Development helps us to push back against this, to encourage teachers to support students in doing something that they are not sure students are capable of accomplishing on their own, to allow students to make approximations, take risks, and then receive additional support in their ZPD (e.g., Cotton, 1998).

Consider another response to that same student:

TEACHER: Thank you for sharing this. I hear that you have probably had a real experience in your own house that has led you to make this argument. This is a reasonable argument for a student to make, and over the years I have heard many students make it. How can you make it clear that this paper is one that only you could have written, that comes from your own experiences? Do you have any ideas, from our classroom discussions, my modeling, or other things you may have read, how an author can make his or her work unique?

STUDENT: When you wrote in front of us, you thought back to something that had happened to you, I guess?

TEACHER: Just think about this for a moment . . . this is a hard concept that I don't expect you to be able to understand without some time to think about it. I am going to send you back to your desk to do just that. Now please repeat back to me what you heard me say. What do you think you should work on when you go back to your seat?

STUDENT: I am going to think about how to make this paper seem like it is only my argument.

TEACHER: And this may be hard, so you are going to slow down and really think, maybe even do some writing before going back to this draft. I am so looking forward to hearing the next version!

An interaction such as this would give the teacher the opportunity to stretch the student's writing ability by asking her to think about a concept that writers must consider, namely, creating unique texts even from less than unique topics. The task may be a stretch for this student, and surely requires some confidence on the part of the teacher. This confidence comes from her knowledge that while the student may not be able to act effectively on this advice, she will still learn from attempting to respond to it. While the first interaction most likely will directly result in a change to the paper that will have risen out of the conversation, the second interaction may not have that same direct effect. The student may take some days, weeks, or several more papers to understand the difficult concept of writing a paper that is unique and specific to her own context. In Lucy Calkins's terms, the teacher in the second example is teaching the writer, not the writing (1994). While the first conference may feel more comfortable to teachers and may provide more satisfaction, since its results will be clear, the second is a much more robust lesson. The good and the bad of robust lessons is that the student may not reveal that she has learned this lesson until time has passed and she encounters other writing tasks. It is harder for students and teachers to count the second conference as a productive learning opportunity, but it is just that (Newkirk, 1995). The teacher planted an important seed of a concept (that writing should be specific to a writer), and asked the student to go off and consider it carefully, and then attempt to implement it in her writing. (Much more specific detail on the way stretch conferences affect student writers will come in Chapters 2, 5 and 6.)

We believe that both of the above interactions would prompt student growth in writing. We think, however, that the first interaction would prompt superficial growth; the second, deep, writerly growth.

RECONSIDERING THE READING CONFERENCE

The same concepts hold true when classroom attention turns to reading, as it does in the following interaction:

> STUDENT (reads): "Flamingos are famous for their bright pink feathers, stilt-like legs and S-shaped neck. They are also known for 'running' on water, thanks to their webbed feet, to gain speed before lifting up into the sky. You'll find flamingos throughout the world's warmer regions, near shallow lakes and lagoons."
>
> TEACHER: Okay, I am going to stop you there. What did you learn about a flamingo that you didn't know before?
>
> STUDENT: That they run on water?
>
> TEACHER: Excellent. Were there any words you didn't know?
>
> STUDENT: *Stilt-like.*
>
> TEACHER: Yes, a stilt is like a long wooden thing that you sometimes see people in parades walking with. Have you ever been to a parade where there was someone up high on big wooden things? Those are stilts.
>
> STUDENT: Oh.

This is a typical interaction between a fluent 4th-grade reader and his teacher. While introducing this student to a new word isn't a bad thing, the teacher might infer that this word is one on which most 4th-graders would stumble. It is one that adds detail, certainly, but that detail is also available through the picture provided as support for the text. We might note that the teacher could have scaffolded the student into figuring out the word on his own, by, for example, directing him to the picture or to knowledge he might already have about flamingos from other readings or visits to the zoo. These adjustments might have yielded a more complex interaction, but still a limited one. This student has no doubt been taught these lessons before. He has been receiving instruction long enough to have been shown how to activate knowledge, how to use pictures, and how to make an inference about an unknown word. Also, he may very well have done these things on his own, given a little more time and the absence of a teacher conveniently sitting with him, telling him to do them. We believe this kind of teacher-student interaction is typical of a reading conference and well intentioned but, like the first writing conference example above, doesn't honor the complexities of the reading process (e.g., Beers & Probst, 2012; García, Pearson, Taylor, Bauer, & Stahl, 2011). We want the interactions between the teacher and the student, when it is just the two of them, to be richer and more distinct (again, considering the notions of approximation and ZPD), and more likely to help students meet the increased demands of the new standards. Note the difference in the stretch conference below:

TEACHER: You read that really well, though I noticed you were reading quite quickly. There is a lot of information packed into a short piece of text. Why do you think the author chose the information he did?

STUDENT: To describe a flamingo.

TEACHER: I think so, too, but I have another question. I wonder what the relationship is between the physical characteristics of the flamingo and their habitat, because for some reason, the author included both of these in one paragraph. This isn't an easy question. You're going to need to stop and think about it. Feel free to use any strategy that you know, including rereading.

STUDENT: Uh, okay.

In the excerpt above, the teacher asks the student to do something that will be hard. His response indicates that he may not know exactly what the teacher wants as an outcome of his reading. While many teachers would continue to push on this, to teach and talk until the student has given assurance of understanding, a stretch conference is defined by suggestions that cause thinking rather than aim at solutions to a particular literacy challenge. The thinking resulting from this interaction may not be demonstrated right then and there. The conference is successful if the student returns to the next reading with some notion that authors sometimes force the reader to make relational inferences that aren't always overtly noted. A rich reading of this text would include the understanding that the animal's characteristics and habitats are interwoven. It would also demonstrate the larger issue regarding reading what is in the text and what is suggested by the text. This lesson is greater than just this text and makes this a piece of reading that adds to a student's scientific knowledge base in deeper ways than just knowing a fact or two about a flamingo. It is also the kind of interaction that really stretches a student's reading, as it is a lesson that can be taken to the next text, and the next. While the student in the first case did learn the meaning of *stilt-like,* he gained very little that would transfer to a future task.

It is counterintuitive to think that learning something concrete in a particular interaction is a barrier to higher-level thinking. We don't think it is as simple as that, of course. We do, however, believe that simple, directed feedback can get in the way of complex thinking, as it can suggest to students that all reading and writing experiences have immediate solutions (Block, 1993; Duke & Pearson, 2002; Sperling, 1991; Stahl, 1998). We know that students need to work on word-level issues in reading and writing, and that accumulating such skills does contribute positively to student outcomes. We don't see, however, the kind of higher-level literacy learning that serves to empower students currently being taught extensively in many literacy classrooms. Without ignoring some prerequisite skills, we are interested in privileging this crucial component in the repertoire of strategies upper elementary and middle grade teachers have for working with students on reading and writing.

CONTINUUM OF TASK COMPLEXITY
FOR GUIDED READING AND WRITING CONFERENCES

Our analysis of the interactions teachers have with students during guided reading reveals that teachers tend to focus mostly on word-level concerns such as decoding or vocabulary, or sentence-level comprehension questions that place very low-level demands on their students' reading. During writing conferences, similarly, teachers tend to focus on low-level revisions (or editing concerns) that demand very little of their writers. (These observations are confirmed by the research of VanDeWeghe, 2007, and Wilson-Powers, 1999.) Based on these observations, we have created a Continuum of Task Complexity During Writing Conferences (described in Chapter 2) and a Continuum of Task Complexity During Reading Conferences (described in Chapter 3). We believe that these continua will help teachers identify their own interactions with students and provide a means for considering how to increase the complexity of those interactions.

In stretch conferences teachers talk individually with students about complex ideas and strategies that will contribute to their proficiency in reading and writing, and they see these conferences as part of a much longer conversation that spans the years of student literacy development. To do this important work, a teacher must have in place classroom management (Anderson, Evertson, & Brophy, 1979), a solid pedagogy for high-quality whole-group instruction (Parsons, 2012), and the understanding that the high-level literacy skills demanded by the Common Core State Standards, as well as other educational mandates, do not come in a snap (Connor et al., 2009). Further, teachers need the support of a strong administrative team that understands this as well (Blachowicz, Fisher, & Ogle, 2006; Blachowicz, Obrochta, & Fogelberg, 2005; Lenz, Ehren, & Deshler, 2005; Raphael & Au, 2005). With these things in mind, we have structured the rest of the book in the following way:

Part I, Chapters 2 and 3, provides an overview of conferences during writing workshop and guided reading, and will help teachers to see how they can use the Continuum of Task Complexity as they begin to analyze their own one-on-one interactions with students.

In particular, they will see how the Continuum provides a heuristic for engaging in stretch conferences that demand more complex thinking from their students.

Part II, Chapters 4 through 6, focuses on writing workshop as the context for one-on-one interactions. Chapter 4 provides a summary of the role of conferences in a writing workshop classroom, while Chapter 5 describes the structure of the actual conference. Chapter 6 provides numerous examples of writing stretch conferences as they have played out in real classrooms. Chapter 4 offers help to teachers who are still making room for process writing in their classrooms, while teachers who already comfortably use and manage a writing workshop approach may want to skip to Chapters 5 and 6, which focus more closely on stretch conferences in writing.

Part III, Chapters 7 through 9, focuses on guided reading as a context for one-on-one interactions. Chapter 7 offers help for teachers who are still unclear about why or how to make room for guided reading in their classrooms, as it addresses how guided reading fits into the literacy block, and provides procedures for simplifying work with small groups and individual students. Chapter 8 looks more closely at the teacher-student interaction during guided reading and helps teachers better understand how to best utilize their time to highlight one-on-one interactions that stretch their students' thinking about reading. Chapter 9 provides real-life examples of and discussion about stretch conferences during guided reading.

Finally, Chapter 10 considers the journey of teacher professional development around stretch conferences and the necessary conditions for making meaningful changes to teacher practice, including time, administrative support, and peer collaboration.

UNDERSTANDING TASK COMPLEXITY

This book discusses conferences in support of both reading and writing. We agree with the many literacy professionals who see reading and writing as complementary processes, but we also believe that there are times to separate them instructionally. For clarity, we have elected to discuss them in different chapters. Chapter 2 introduces stretch conferences teachers enact during writing instruction. Chapter 3 discusses reading conferences. Taken together, the two chapters present a conceptual model for complex talk about complex texts, either written by or read by students. We embed these conferences in a balanced literacy classroom that includes both writing workshop and guided reading. In Chapters 4 and 7, we review the elements of full models of writing and of reading instruction, respectively. Conferences are but one component of these two instructional models. Some readers may prefer to learn more about writing workshop prior to diving into the discussion of writing conferences. If so, they may wish to read Chapter 4 before Chapter 2. Readers who prefer to learn more about guided reading prior to the discussion of reading conferences may wish to read Chapters 7 and 8 before Chapter 3.

Stretch Conferences and the Continuum of Task Complexity in Writing

As noted in Chapter 1, a stretch conference is a one-on-one interaction between student and teacher where the goal is to stretch a student's understanding of reading or writing. It is distinguished from conferences where the focus is on improving the quality of the paper at hand or privileging understanding of a particular text.

The goal of teachers engaged in writing stretch conferences is to teach for future writing improvement. In order to do so, a teacher will have to prioritize particular aspects of writing, overlooking others. This is always difficult for teachers, who, understandably, want to help students with as much as they possibly can at a given moment. Clearly, though, when students are given too much direction, too many things to which they must attend, they often feel overwhelmed. They often attend to the simpler concern and not to the more complicated one. It is always simpler to give a specific and contained piece of advice to a writer (e.g., add some detail here) than it is to ask students to think about a less specific and contained, less directive aspect of their paper (e.g., I wonder what your purpose for writing this might be?). These more amorphous comments, however, change writers, not just writing.

In order to help teachers focus upon those things that really make a difference for a writer, we have designed a continuum that includes both more and less complex aspects of writing (Figure 2.1). As teachers look at the continuum from left to right, they will note that the boxes describe important characteristics of student writing instruction. This continuum is designed, not necessarily as a visual representation of what a student will move through, but rather as a

Figure 2.1. Continuum of Task Complexity During Writing Conferences

Level 1	Level 2	Level 3	Level 4a	Level 4b	Level 5
Mechanics	Changing a word or phrase	Adding or taking away details	Uniqueness	Organizing to support a particular genre	Why does this matter?

tool for teachers who wish to use conferences to increase the complexity of their responses to student writers. It is not intended to value some aspects of writing instruction over others, but rather to point to those aspects that are more complicated so that teachers might make choices about when to emphasize particular pieces of instruction. Teachers who note students struggling with elements at the lower end of the continuum will attend to those, but likely can do so in contexts other than one-on-one conferences.

While Levels 1, 2, and 3 are necessary, they generally can be taught to the whole group (and by the time students get to the middle grades, often already have been taught and need now to be reinforced). The instructional elements of Levels 4a, 4b, and 5 can be taught to the whole group as well, but because they are the more complicated and contextual lessons, they are most effective if taught by the teacher in response to students' individual writing. Recalling the example conference in Chapter 1, teachers can prompt change in a paper by, for instance, asking a student to use interesting language. Over time, a writer might learn that spicing up language creates more interest for a reader. But we have seen that particular lesson taught very effectively in a whole-group setting using minilessons, directed exercises, and lots of student writing practice. The precious time a teacher can devote to an individual student's writing needs can be best spent on the elements of writing that fall on the right side of the continuum.

When teachers dig deeply into an individual student's paper, they find elements that are difficult to teach when decontextualized from that paper. This may sound as if it contradicts the previous point about focusing not on a particular piece of writing but on the writer, but it does not. When teachers analyze pieces of student writing, it helps them to see what students are not yet doing as writers and presents a teaching opportunity directly tied to student performance. The papers are artifacts of student ability, and so they become the data teachers use to determine the next steps for students. This is akin to the teacher of a young student doing a running record and using the student's oral reading to plan future instruction. In a writing conference, the teacher can give the student immediate feedback at a complex level, and note the need for future instruction, perhaps in the areas representing Levels 1–3, perhaps in the other levels. Below is the kind of conversation that we often have with teachers as we coach them in working with students on their writing:

> **COMMON CORE CONNECTION**
>
> The Writing Anchor Standards for Grades 6–12 state: "For students, writing is a key means of asserting and defending claims, showing what they know about a subject, and conveying what they have experienced, imagined, thought, and felt. To be college- and career ready writers, students must take task, purpose, and audience into careful consideration, choosing words, information, structures, and formats deliberately. They need to know how to combine elements of different kinds of writing—for example, to use narrative strategies within argument and explanation within narrative—to produce complex and nuanced writing."
>
> These expectations cannot be met if we focus our attention on lower-level concerns.

Us: I could tell that you were really listening to Jordan as he read. And I agree that it was pretty clear that he rushed through the details of the actual basketball game. However, I am not sure that adding more about the game will actually solve the fundamental writing problem.

Teacher: Which is . . . ?

Us: I think that there actually wasn't anything special about this game, at least nothing he noted. I am not sure exactly why he wrote it, what he was trying to communicate. All the detail on the game in the world likely won't clarify that.

Teacher: Yes, and maybe I would tell him both of those things.

Us: The clarity of purpose, however, is so important that establishing that might give the piece a whole new emphasis. Until then, it won't be clear what should be expanded.

This teacher was very careful to make decisions in her original conference about changes she believed would improve this paper. She was correct that adding detail to the events might make it a bit livelier. However, without a clear distinguishable purpose, this paper might get "better," but it will likely never get really good.

This teacher, like all of us, will have to forgo the immediate gratification of giving this student a clear piece of feedback, knowing that he can likely use it, and instead offer a comment that will prompt thinking, but will not be as easily executed by the student. Of course, this will have implications for assessment, a topic that we will discuss in future chapters.

First, we explain the levels of the continuum and their role in student writing growth.

LEVEL 1: MECHANICS

Mechanics have an important role in student writing. Correcting writing so that it is presented in a polished manner is an important step in the writing process, but it is one among many. Because it has traditionally taken more than its fair share of emphasis, many teachers are careful to instruct students to plan, draft, get feedback, and revise without focusing on correct Standard Written English. Students learn to focus their attention on issues of grammar and mechanics when they are preparing the paper for submission. In the editing and proofreading stage of the writing process, students use the tools they have learned to examine their papers for errors and correct them to the best of their best abilities. Part of writing process instruction is helping students distinguish when it is appropriate to work on mechanics and when they should concentrate on the content of the paper.

In addition, we work with teachers on developing the discipline required to work with students (especially those who struggle) on the more content-related elements of writing even if mechanics are the "presenting" problem. If teachers always go to grammar, spelling, and usage first, students who struggle never get the rich instruction that comes from considering the many other elements involved in good writing. Nonetheless, when working with students, we have ourselves had to sit on our hands not to circle egregious errors in order to keep the focus on higher-level concerns. Teachers may feel tempted to work on elements that students can incorporate immediately, resulting in an improved paper. However, students don't learn how to correct their writing in an instant. Grammar, syntax, and orthographic knowledge are cumulative and improve over time with practice in authentic contexts (Calkins, 1980; Smith, Cheville, & Hillocks, 2006). Simply pointing out an error or even quickly explaining a rule will not usually do much more than offer a quick, superficial fix.

We suggest that a writing conference is never the site for working on mechanical concerns. Often teachers feel guilty, or as if they aren't teaching well, if a student presents them with a paper riddled with mechanical errors and they do not say anything. As a remedy, it has been our habit to say quietly to ourselves, "Like all students, there are many things that this student needs to be taught, but I am not going to teach her that today." This frees us to teach her something else instead. Consider the following conference.

Student reads her piece aloud:

What do you think makes a good friend, have you ever thought that you were a bad friend? Well if you have a friend who is rude to you and makes fun of you all the time then you probably don't want to be their friend. A good friend is a friend who is nice to you and respects you for who you are. If you have a friend that is mean and judges you by what you're wearing or doing, they are probably not a good friend.

TEACHER: I really like this piece. You seem to have a strong sense of what makes a good friend. I like how you started your paper with a question, but that opening seems to be a little long. Perhaps dividing it into two sentences will help. Do you think you can do that?

Is the teacher wrong? No. But she shows, through this feedback, that what she values most is correctness. Consider what will happen after this interaction. The student will go back to her desk and decide that she should use a question mark instead of a comma between her opening sentences. After that, she will have completed the task, and she may decide that the piece is done. The content of this piece will not have improved a bit, and this student will have moved no further toward understanding how to be a more effective writer than she was before.

When students interrupt the drafting/feedback/revision component of the writing process to work on editing, their cognitive energy is split. Students should focus on mechanics in the editing phase of the writing process, when the content work is done. This doesn't mean that teachers should not note when a student is struggling with, for example, sentence fragments or subject/verb agreement. A writing conference allows teachers to collect multiple data points about student writing at the same time. However, collecting these data and emphasizing them during the conference are two different things. With struggling students, and, often, English language learners, teachers could work on the mechanical elements of writing endlessly. If they turn to them during one-on-one conferences, they will likely cover nothing else, limiting these students' learning to editing only.

Teachers often ask if they should just mark student errors during the conference and not comment on them. In our experience, doing so draws attention to something that we hope will not be of concern during the conference. We therefore urge teachers to keep what they note about student errors to themselves, to work on at another time.

LEVEL 2: CHANGING A WORD OR PHRASE

Another common type of feedback involves asking students to reconsider their word choice. Many writing standards, across the grades, indicate that appropriate word choice is a characteristic of good student writing. We agree, and we have seen brilliant whole-group instruction in support of this. Nonetheless, noting a weak word or two in a given paper has minimal impact both on the quality of the piece and on the student's understanding of good writing.

Consider this response to the same student's (above) writing.

TEACHER: I really like this piece. You seem to have a strong sense of what makes a good friend. You know, *makes fun* is a little vague. Do you mean *tease*? Or do you know another word that is more concrete?

STUDENT: No, I guess I mean *tease*.

TEACHER: Why don't you make that change, then, in order to clarify what you mean, okay?

Though one could argue that this is a more meaningful interaction than the earlier, more mechanics-oriented exchange, it still is likely to have little impact on this student's piece, less the replacement of one word. Furthermore, this student is not likely to take anything from this interaction that will help her when she's writing her next piece. She may change *makes fun* to *tease*, but she doesn't take away an understanding of why *tease* is better, or what it does, if anything, to make the piece stronger.

Recall the example in Chapter 1 of a teacher who asked a student to select a more vivid word as she argued for doing away with her bedtime. Remember that we agreed that this might very well be a better word choice and thus improve the paper. We also agree that repeated feedback of this sort on student writing might lead to improvement in students' independent, unprompted use of descriptive words. However, this element of writing is easily noted by a peer group and, actually, a good thing to have students look for when they exchange papers for feedback. We will talk more about the way peer interactions function in a balanced literacy classroom in future chapters. Peers really are able to note dull words and request others, especially when there has been some whole-group discussion regarding what makes certain words more vivid than others. This is a lesson that students can learn in many different contexts in the classroom; thus we avoid discussion of it during more specialized one-on-one interactions. Teachers often throw in a comment about avoiding dull words or trite phrases at the end of a stretch conference. This, like a nag about spelling or grammar, tends to distract from the hard thinking that we hope to prompt.

LEVEL 3: ADDING OR TAKING AWAY DETAILS

It is not usually difficult to dissuade teachers from tackling the first two levels on the continuum during writing conferences. They generally understand why mechanics or word-level changes to writing are low-level fixes that do not tend to have a meaningful impact on students' writing. However, Level 3 feedback, focused on adding important information or taking away redundant or unnecessary information, occurs frequently in the conferences we observe. Teachers appear to feel comfortable providing this kind of feedback, both because it is something they understand well and because it often leads to changes in student writing that are both noticeable and satisfying.

In our earlier years teaching writing we, too, frequently uttered the words, "Can you give me more detail?" This was a fail-safe, go-to response that made us feel as if we were helping students make their papers better. We now see that this feedback resulted in the same paper that the student had brought to the conference, but now with more detail. It didn't change the way the student understood writing, and it didn't fundamentally alter the bones of the paper. It is true that, like attention to words, repeated direction to add more detail and to show, not tell, usually does eventually convert to an independent skill. Some students are more successful than others because they have noted models in their own reading or have had previous instruction. Most students can improve their attention to detail with the examination of mentor texts that are very descriptive, and with an indication of descriptive detail's importance on a rubric. That is to say, this, too, is most efficiently taught as part of whole-class instruction.

Below is an example of a conference that makes Level 3 difficulty demands.

> TEACHER: I like what you have to say about friendship. This topic seems to matter to you very much. I'm wondering if you could help me understand more about your bad friend by describing her. What does she look like? How does her voice sound?
> STUDENT: Yes, I can do that.
> TEACHER: I think that would help us better understand what you mean by being a bad friend.

Let's imagine that this student goes back to her desk and adds a description of her bad friend. She might even be motivated to add other details. This is very gratifying for student and teacher alike, as the teacher believes she has made an impact on the student's writing with her feedback, and the student can see a tangible difference between her first and second draft. The student adds a description; however, she doesn't necessarily gain an understanding of why this makes her writing better, or why a description would be useful here instead of in another spot in her piece. In other words, she doesn't put herself in her audience's shoes to consider how she may need to clarify her meaning for her reader. Instead, she follows directions.

The next three categories require more from both teacher and student, as they delve into the complexities of good writing and the considerations an author must make when writing. We have included a Level 4a and a Level 4b, because we don't believe that one is necessarily more complex than the other, just different. Teachers will make choices to attend to one or the other based upon the paper the student produces and their understanding of the student as a writer.

LEVEL 4A: UNIQUE QUALITIES

In this level, teachers consider what it is about a student's writing that marks it as his own. Voice is part of it, but voice is not the only feature to mark a paper as unique. How does an author distinguish his work from someone else's? Never an easy thing for students to understand, uniqueness can be, similarly, a challenge for teachers to teach. Teachers can begin to approach the challenge by helping students reflect upon what makes their writing distinct. Is it humor? The use of figurative language? A specific opinion? A past experience? Specialized knowledge? Teachers might explain to students that what they say should be a learning experience for their readers. If they make the same argument that others have made over and over, what is the purpose of reading their papers? All writers should consider how their writing can present a unique spin, even on a less-than-unique topic.

Consider this teacher's Level 4a feedback during the conference.

TEACHER: I'm really interested in this topic, but I need to know that you have something to say about this that is specific to you. If everybody in this class wrote on this same topic and nobody put their names on it, how would I know that it was yours? That is a funny way to think about it, but if everyone's ended up the same, what good would they be?

STUDENT: Well, from the examples I give?

TEACHER: Could be. What is it about yourself that you would like to show through in your writing? That's a hard question, and you don't have to tell me now, but when you go back to your desk, give it some thought. Your goal is to mark this as yours so there is no question it is from you and only you.

Notice that in this situation, the teacher encourages the student to do something she is not sure the student can do. Her feedback is less direct than it would be in Levels 1, 2, or 3, more nebulous. Some teachers feel very uncomfortable with this kind of feedback because they don't feel as if they've directly impacted the quality of the student's writing if they haven't provided explicit and easy-to-execute feedback. Yet this is exactly the notion of approximation (e.g., Calkins, 2003; Cambourne, 1988) that scholars believe is the path toward deep learning. In this interaction, the teacher has given the student an invitation to try something new, to take a risk with her writing. Even if it doesn't work with the current piece, the teacher knows that this is a forever lesson; through it, the student can learn that the writer should always strive for a unique position relative to a topic.

> **COMMON CORE CONNECTION**
>
> The Anchor Standards for Writing 1–3 focus on Level 4b concerns, as they ask students to consider the different text types (Argument, Informative, and Narrative), and when and how they are used.

LEVEL 4B: ORGANIZING TO SUPPORT A GENRE

Different genres require different approaches on the part of the writer. Each genre achieves its purpose through a particular organizational structure and knowledge of organizational distinctions can help as students attempt to write successfully in different genres. The teacher in the example below works with a student on this very element, represented by Level 4b on the continuum.

TEACHER: I'm trying to figure out if you're trying to convince me, you're telling me a story, or you're trying to describe something. Do you know what you're trying to do with this piece? What is your purpose in writing it, and what are some things you can do to let me know?

STUDENT: That's a good question! I started out by trying to describe what a good friend is, but now that you ask me that, I kind of wonder if I'm trying to convince you that good friends will act a certain way.

TEACHER: I appreciate understanding your thinking. When you go back to your desk to work on this, be mindful of your purpose. What are you trying to do with this piece? Once you figure it out, consider changes you might make in order to make it clear why you're writing this. The changes may have to do with reordering and they may have to do with adding. Remember, if you are making an argument, you have to have supports. If you are teaching the reader something, then you have to take them carefully through your points. If you are telling a story, you need detail and description to engage the reader. I'm not sure which way you will go. That is up to you as the writer.

This interaction is particularly effective because it contains instruction on the way decisions about genre help student writers. While many teachers work with students to understand genre in many different ways, they almost always teach the lesson prior to student writing. In this case, the teacher is able to show her student the way in which a consideration of genre defines the paper and its function. So much of instruction around genre defines the task for students before they have had a chance to see what they might want to do with a piece of writing. It is understandable, given standards and high-stakes testing, that teachers will want students to have experiences writing in a variety of genres and will want to share the particular characteristics of them (i.e., claim, warrant, evidence in an argumentative paper; comparison/contrast in an expository paper). However, students must also be able to determine their own genre based on what they want to communicate and to whom. Like the interaction before this one, the student has a lot of decisions to make, but the teacher has set the path for that decisionmaking, allowing for the possibility of growth.

LEVEL 5: WHY DOES THIS MATTER?

This final category need not sound cavalier or dismissive of our students' writing. When students put pen to paper, they are often extremely committed to their topics; those topics matter very much to them. Other times, though, when students begin to write they may be just going through the motions. The feedback described below is meant to fight back against complacency. What is important about the writing? Why does it matter? With so many papers to read, why should someone want to read this one? The teacher in the example below discusses this with the student.

> TEACHER: I do like the way you've described friends, both good and bad. I have a question for you, though. You don't have to answer right away. Does this piece matter to you? I mean really matter?
> STUDENT: Yes. I feel like I have a lot to say about friendship.
> TEACHER: I'm glad to hear that. You know what I'd like to understand a little bit better? I am curious: What about this made you really want to write it, and what would make me really want to read it? You don't have to answer right away. But when you go back to your desk, please think about how this paper could stand out to make it really matter in this class, in this school, and in the world. What are you helping us to see about friendship that others haven't been able to write or haven't written this way?

As with the Level 4a and 4b prompts, in a Level 5 prompt there is not an easy answer to teacher-posed questions. The teacher demands much more of the student than she may be confident that the student can handle. Thus, she is not sure what the student's next draft will look like—if it will be different, or if it will be better. But she is again allowing the student to take risks with her writing, to try to change her piece in such a way that it is clearly distinct and meaningful in the world. This has to be the ultimate goal for our writers: to write things that really matter. Adding a period, changing a word, or even adding a specific example, though part of good writing, will not help a student get closer to writing things that really matter.

TO SUMMARIZE

In reflecting on this chapter, return to the continuum in Figure 2.1 to consider how a teacher's language, agenda, and expectations change, depending upon the focus of the feedback. On the left end, there is low demand/high expectation of success. At the right end, there is high demand/lower expectation of success. As we acknowledged before, working at the right end of the continuum can be very unsettling for both student and teacher. Nonetheless, a steady diet of low demands probably won't offer students all that powerful writing can offer them.

The continuum is a heuristic that assists teachers in focusing upon elements that are difference-makers, that direct student writers' thinking rather than directing them to make a specific change to a single paper. Though the heuristic is a helpful guide, much of the success in converting a regular conference into one that stretches student thinking comes from experience. In the final chapter, we discuss the ways in which teachers can work together to continually reflect upon and improve their skills. It is hard to do this without plenty of practice, plenty of talk, and the opportunity to reflect with colleagues.

Chapters 4 and 5 offer a structure for writing instruction that has proven successful for many teachers as they prioritize conferences with students. As stated in the beginning of this chapter, teachers must embed conferences within other instructional practices that support writing development, such as attention to mentor texts, minilessons, teacher modeling, peer feedback, time for independent writing, and instruction in grammar, syntax, and spelling.

Teachers who are comfortable with their work related to setting up, managing, and maintaining strong writing instruction in a writing workshop context may want to skip Chapter 4, which goes into detail on that. Chapter 5 is a complete description of the writing conference, and in Chapter 6 we offer many more examples of quality writing conferences.

CHAPTER 3

Stretch Conferences and the Continuum of Task Complexity in Guided Reading

Just as we have categorized the kinds of interactions that teachers have with students during writing conferences and placed them on a continuum from less to more complex, so have we categorized the conferences teachers have with students during guided reading. As with writing conferences, we believe that the time teachers spend talking with students during guided reading is extremely valuable. We hope this continuum will assist them as they begin to take full advantage of that time. As in writing, a reading conference is but one interaction in the context of a full complement of experiences that teachers design for students to improve their reading.

Often we see teachers working with upper elementary and middle grade students on decoding or vocabulary issues rather than querying students to determine if they really understand what they have read. This is true even though researchers believe that comprehension ought to be the focus of attention in these grades (Ivey & Baker, 2004; Schoenbach, Greenleaf, & Murphy, 2012). Our debriefing session following our observation of a guided reading group often goes something like this:

> Us: Do you remember when Zoe was reading the paragraph about earthquakes and she got stuck on the word *magma*?
> TEACHER: Yes.
> Us: You helped her to figure out how to pronounce *magma* by chunking it into two syllables and putting them together. That's a great strategy for figuring out a word you don't know

how to pronounce, but do you think she understood what it meant in that sentence and what magma has to do with earthquakes?

TEACHER: I'm not sure. Probably not.

US: What we might do when a student struggles with a word like that is to say something like, "You know, Zoe, that is a word you don't see every day, right? Right now, I'm less concerned that you know how to say it, and more concerned that you can figure out what's going on in this paragraph. What does this word have to do with the surface of the Earth and the way it moves?"

TEACHER: But won't that be hard for Zoe if she doesn't even know what that word is?

US: It might be hard for her to answer that question, but knowing how to pronounce *magma* isn't likely to make it easier.

We have such conversations frequently, and we think we understand why. Teachers want their students to be successful. Success can be more readily attained with a fix that is easy for the student. Decoding issues are often easily fixable, and the results are immediate. The student can read a new word when he leaves the table, and both teacher and student feel satisfied. However, interactions that only look at word-level concerns may send our students, especially struggling readers, the message that reading is about figuring out hard words. This is borne out by interviews with students (Degener & Berne, n.d.), who indicate that a good reader knows how to read "long words." Instead, students need to know that a good reader is someone who can utilize strategies, when necessary, to make sense of text.

THE CONTINUUM OF TASK COMPLEXITY DURING GUIDED READING

In order to help teachers focus on student meaning-making, we categorized student-teacher interactions according to their level of complexity. For example, during classroom observations we saw that many interactions revolved around a specific word within the

Figure 3.1. Continuum of Task Complexity During Reading Conferences

Level 1	Level 2	Level 3	Level 4	Level 5	Level 6
Word-level decoding	Word-level vocabulary	Sentence-level comprehension	Cumulative comprehension	Critical consideration	Discerning greater meaning

text that the student struggled to read or understand. We categorized these as "word-level" concerns. We categorized other interactions as addressing "sentence-level" concerns, in cases where teachers asked literal comprehension questions that required students to make sense of a specific sentence. More complex interactions were categorized as "cumulative comprehension" (to reflect the activity of thinking across a text), "critical understanding" (an activity that would require students not just to understand, but also to critique), and finally, "discerning greater meaning" (a highly sophisticated kind of reading that involves placing the text in dialogue with the world). In categorizing interactions according to complexity, we have drawn on Raphael's (1982, 1986) notion of Question-Answer Relationships (QAR). Figure 3.1 shows a more specific look at these interactions along a continuum from least to most complex. In the remainder of the chapter, we discuss each level and how it contributes to a student's literacy growth.

LEVEL 1: WORD-LEVEL DECODING

Guided reading in the primary grades, for students just learning to read, most often focuses on word-level concerns. Kindergarten and 1st-grade teachers know that beginning readers must concentrate on "cracking the code." Interactions with early readers involve helping students to invoke decoding strategies (e.g., "chunk it" or "look at the beginning sound and look at the picture") in order to figure out unknown words. Still, we encourage primary grade teachers to call their beginning readers' attention to meaning-making by first asking, "Does that make sense?" In this way, teachers are building the notion of meaning-making as being of primary importance.

As students become more fluent readers, guided reading serves them best when it is centered on meaning-making. However, we know that teachers want to provide support for *all* of the challenges students face. It can be difficult to ignore decoding issues, particularly when students are so used to getting teacher support in reading challenging words. Following is an example of a teacher-student interaction during guided reading that focuses on decoding (Level 1) concerns.

Text says: *Bacteria are microscopic organisms that are too small to see or feel. There are five million trillion trillion bacteria on Earth, and they are literally everywhere, from the top of Mount Everest to the deepest trench in the Pacific Ocean. You are surrounded by them right now, and your body is filled with them. The majority of bacteria are harmless. Many are actually crucial to our survival, like the bacteria that line our intestines and help us digest our food. (From Scholastic Scope, January 2014, p. 6)*

Student reads the first two sentences mostly accurately, but says "organs" instead of "organisms."

Teacher stops the student, points to the word *organisms*, and says, "I heard you pronounce this word as *organs*. I understand why, because look [she covers up the end of the word]: This word begins with the letters of *organ*. Let's cover up *organ* and look at the rest of the word. What do you see?

STUDENT: "isms"?
TEACHER: Great, now put those two parts together.
STUDENT: Organ-isms?
TEACHER: You've got it, now say it again.

We understand why a teacher might focus the conversation in this way. She might feel that the student can't possibly be making sense of this passage if he says "organs" instead of "organisms." She might know that this student often has accuracy problems, and she may feel strongly that his accuracy must be addressed. She may also feel confident that she can help him read the word correctly, and she knows the importance of building the student's self-esteem during reading. Whatever the reason, we would ask this teacher to resist the push to address accuracy during guided reading.

LEVEL 2: WORD-LEVEL VOCABULARY

Vocabulary and comprehension are connected, and we know that students who have larger vocabularies tend to have an easier time with reading comprehension. Awareness of this connection may be the reason that teachers want students to understand each and every word they read. For some students, particularly struggling readers and English language learners, guided reading interactions frequently center on vocabulary issues, because teachers fear that if students don't know what words mean, they will not be able to make sense of the text.

Consider how the interaction above might have gone had the teacher focused on vocabulary instead of decoding.

> TEACHER (holding finger under *organisms*): I heard you say *organs* for this word. Take another look, making sure you look at the last part of the word, too.
>
> STUDENT: Oh, I mean *organisms*.
>
> TEACHER: Good! Now, I wonder if you know what that word means.
>
> STUDENT: Not really.
>
> TEACHER: Well, what vocabulary strategy that we have learned about might help you figure out the meaning of that word?
>
> STUDENT: I could look at the words around it?
>
> TEACHER: Sure, try that.
>
> STUDENT: Well, it says that a bacteria is a microscopic organism, so I guess bacteria and organism are kind of the same, only maybe an organism isn't necessarily tiny?
>
> TEACHER: Good. I like the way you looked at the other words in the sentence to figure that out.

Note that the teacher didn't focus exclusively on the pronunciation of *organism*, and instead directed most of the interaction to the meaning of the word, increasing the complexity of the interaction. However, we encourage teachers to consider the possibility that sometimes it is okay not to understand the meaning of every word. Truthfully, in the context of guided reading, it may be impossible for the student to discern the meaning of certain words, even while utilizing multiple vocabulary strategies. Context clues, for example, are useful only a portion of the time. Using word parts (affixes) or knowledge of Greek and Latin roots can be helpful, but doesn't guarantee that a student will figure out the word, either. In such cases, teachers often spend precious guided reading time helping students tap into strategies that don't necessarily help in that situation, and fail to bring students closer to understanding the overall meaning of the text. Indeed, in the above scenario, the student took a plausible stab at the meaning of *organism*, but didn't in fact provide an accurate definition for it.

What would have happened if the teacher had not asked the student to define the word *organism?* Is it still possible for the student to understand the meaning of the passage without knowing that word? We believe it is possible, and further, we know that capable readers often read and make sense of passages even when they don't know the meaning of every word.

We also worry that English language learners, who understandably have smaller English vocabularies, could work on vocabulary issues ad infinitum and may never get to the point where they are held accountable for making meaning of an entire passage or text, instead of just the vocabulary therein.

LEVEL 3: SENTENCE-LEVEL COMPREHENSION

A focus on comprehension isn't always analogous with complexity. Questions that require students to reread one sentence or to remember the details of just a small portion of the material do not demand much from students. Though teachers certainly should want students to recall simple information from texts, it is important to understand that comprehension doesn't begin and end with factual recall, and recall questions are not sufficient for checking students' complete understanding of a text.

Consider, again, the passage about bacteria from above. In this situation, the child has read the text more or less correctly.

TEACHER: You read that very well. Do you remember how many bacteria there are on Earth?

STUDENT: Boy, I remember there was a lot, but I don't remember how many.

TEACHER: What's one thing a reader can do when they don't remember something from what they've read?

STUDENT: They can go back and look in the text?

TEACHER: Of course! Please do that and see if you can find the answer.

STUDENT: Oh, here it is. There are five million trillion trillion bacteria.

TEACHER: Good job. I like the way you looked back at the text and found the answer.

In this scenario, the student has demonstrated that he can go back to the text to find the answer to a question. That is an important ability for students that will help on standardized tests, and in answering questions at the ends of chapters in social studies and science. However, a child who is asked only these kinds of questions will not understand that making meaning of texts is often complex. And a child's ability to answer these types of questions tells us only that the child can recall information or find a sentence that will answer the question, not that he has the ability to restate or synthesize the information he has read in order to consider the larger meaning.

Teachers may be tempted to ask these types of questions during guided reading. First of all, it is easy to think of sentence-level comprehension questions on the fly. In guided reading, teachers are time-pressed, which often leads them to default to sentence-level questions. Also, it is easier for teachers to assess students' sentence-level understanding than their deeper understanding of a whole passage. If students can answer a basic sentence-level comprehension question, it is tempting to conclude that they understand the text. If they cannot, teachers can easily direct them to reread it.

Each of the interactions we describe above is successful in that it achieves its intended purpose—the teacher helped the student activate a strategy in order to read a word accurately, provide a reasonable definition for a word, or answer a simple question—but in no case was the student given the opportunity to grapple with the whole passage, to demonstrate broader understanding, or to think about the implications of the passage. A student whose interactions with his teacher during guided reading remain focused on Levels 1, 2, or 3 of complexity is not being asked to demonstrate rich understanding or to engage in higher-level thinking. A student would probably not be inclined to think deeply about the texts he reads if he is never expected to do so. By contrast, the next three levels, described below, demand more of students and push them to have a deeper sense of what it means to read and comprehend text.

LEVEL 4: CUMULATIVE COMPREHENSION

Picking out discrete facts from text, though challenging for some students, doesn't require them to read and make sense of an entire piece of text in order to discern its "big picture" meaning. Indeed, when teachers begin to increase the complexity of their questions during guided reading, students

> **COMMON CORE CONNECTION**
>
> Checking students' cumulative understanding allows teachers to ascertain whether or not students are using text evidence in answering questions about it.

often cannot respond appropriately. When an answer isn't readily available in one single location in the text, they often don't know what to do. We have labeled a question that involves holding information from multiple parts of a text (or more than one text) "cumulative comprehension." These questions require students to demonstrate that they can make and refine meaning over the course of one or more texts.

Below are two examples of what might transpire between a student and teacher when the teacher is ascertaining cumulative comprehension of our by-now-familiar bacteria passage.

TEACHER: You just read a lot of information about bacteria. Help me to understand this passage by talking me through the main ideas you just read about.

STUDENT: Well, there are an awful lot of bacteria all over the world.

TEACHER: Yes, but I think there's more to this paragraph. Please help me to understand all the important ideas in there. Feel free to go back and read it to yourself. This time, make sure you're considering all the information you learned about bacteria.

STUDENT (reads to himself for a few moments, and then turns to the teacher): There are trillions and trillions of bacteria everywhere—on top of Mount Everest, and at the very bottom of the ocean. They are all around us and even inside us. And they're not all bad for us. I think it's even saying that they can be good for us. Like they help us digest food?

TEACHER: Good, now I know you really understood what this paragraph was saying.

It can be tempting to settle for surface-level understanding, but such expectations limit students as readers. Students need to hold information from one part of a text to another as they tell teachers about what they just read. Keep in mind that this kind of understanding doesn't come easily for many of our students, particularly for those of whom we have not expected it.

The interaction could just as easily have gone as follows:

TEACHER: You just read a lot of information about bacteria. Help me to understand this passage by talking me through the main ideas you just read about.

STUDENT: Well, there are an awful lot of bacteria all over the world.

TEACHER: Yes, but I think there's more to this paragraph. Please help me to understand all the important ideas in there. Feel free to go back and read it to yourself. This time, make sure you're considering all the information you learned about bacteria.

STUDENT (after reading for a few moments): Okay, well, there are bacteria everywhere. In trenches, on mountains, even inside our bodies. Also, bacteria can make us sick.

TEACHER: It may be true that bacteria can make us sick, but will you please show me where in this paragraph it says that?

STUDENT (pointing to the text): Right here.

TEACHER: Will you read that again, and think about exactly where it says that bacteria can make us sick?

STUDENT (reads again): Oh, actually it says that most bacteria are not bad for us. (Reads some more.) It says that some actually help keep us healthy.

TEACHER: Okay, good . . . remember to read very carefully. When you're reading, it can be hard to sort out what you think you know from what you're reading on the page. When I ask you to tell me about something you've read, make sure you're getting that information from the passage and not from your head!

Attending to the text at hand is a challenge for students, because they must make sure prior knowledge doesn't create a barrier to the way they read and process information. While all readers bring their prior knowledge to any reading, skillful readers understand that background knowledge combines with new learning to create new understandings. In the example above, the student has a sense from something she has previously read or heard that bacteria are bad. Although the paragraph doesn't say that, she allows that incomplete understanding to cloud her meaning-making. Instead of allowing information that she gathers through reading to interact with that which she already knows, she is attempting merely to confirm existing knowledge. Level 4 demands give the teacher significant insight into how students are engaging in close readings, and if they are informing their knowledge base with information gathered during a particular reading. This supports Common Core Reading Anchor Standard 1, which calls for students to use specific textual evidence to support conclusions they draw from the text at hand. Teachers' interactions with students during guided reading are an ideal time to support this capability.

In addition, retaining information from the beginning to the end of the reading can be a challenge. Students may drift mentally as they read, especially if the text at hand is not something that naturally engages their interest. Students may be able to remember one or two facts from their reading, but often struggle to figure out or remember how those facts are connected or how all the information included works together. All readers have had the experience of checking out of a reading for a time. It happens for readers of all levels. Strong readers realize that this is happening and take steps to remedy it. Students need to identify a loss of attention so they can go back and use an available strategy to attend more fully to the text. Noting an inability to successfully answer a question that relies upon a large portion of text can help a teacher work with the student on attending. Note that we do not equate "cumulative comprehension" with summarizing. For some reading tasks, teachers certainly want students to be able to summarize. However, given the new emphasis on rigor, teachers also want to ensure that students can gather deep meaning from a text. Students must understand that summarizing doesn't always capture all that a text has to offer.

LEVEL 5: CRITICAL CONSIDERATION

Sometimes cumulative understanding of texts is all that teachers expect from their students. Other times, they expect students to think about texts in more analytical, critical ways—to do something with the text beyond just demonstrating understanding. This is similar to Rosenblatt's (1994) notion of transaction, or Raphael's (1982, 1986) notion of Author and Me, in that students must consider how their own worldview informs their understanding of the text. The example below shows how a teacher can prompt students to demonstrate this kind of understanding:

TEACHER: What do you think would happen if bacteria were somehow removed from a person's body?

STUDENT: They'd probably be healthier.

TEACHER: What makes you say that?

STUDENT: Well, I know that bacteria can get in our food and make us sick, so if there were no bacteria inside our bodies, then we might be healthier.

TEACHER: You are probably right that some bacteria in our bodies can make us sick, but what in the text makes you say that?

STUDENT (reading to himself): Wait a minute. It actually says that bacteria are crucial to our survival . . . and the bacteria in our intestines help us digest food. I guess the answer to your question is that without bacteria inside of us, we might actually be less healthy. We maybe couldn't digest food without them. The text helped me understand this.

The teacher is asking the student to make a textual inference. Instead, initially, the student draws on what he already knows about the topic. By directing him back to the text, the teacher helps the student understand the intersection between his own experiences and direct textual evidence.

LEVEL 6: DISCERNING GREATER MEANING

Students read a lot in school, and it isn't all interesting or important to them. However, there are times when the things students read matter a great deal in the world at large, and it is important (though challenging) for students to figure out how and why the reading matters in the grand scheme of things. We believe students discern greater meaning when they can position an article or other text within the world outside of their own individual lives and understand its relevance in the world. Students often assume that what they read in school is "school-only," and assign it little or no importance. It can be extremely challenging to get students to think about why they're reading something. In order to tap into this higher level of understanding, a teacher might initiate the following conversation during guided reading:

TEACHER: I want you to consider how this article intersects with the recent phenomenon of making hand soaps and other cleaning products antibacterial.

STUDENT: I'm not sure what you mean.

TEACHER: Well, think about it. What does this paragraph tell us about the majority of bacteria?

STUDENT: That they're everywhere?

TEACHER: That's true, but go back and reread, and think about what this article says about the majority of bacteria and how that fits into our craze to make everything antibacterial.

Clearly, in this situation, the teacher is hoping the student will say something about how, if the majority of bacteria are harmless and some are even crucial to our health, the use of antibacterial products could end up having a negative impact on our health, so why do so many products contain antibacterial ingredients? However, if the student hasn't been asked many questions like this previously during guided reading (or if the focus during guided reading has been at the word level), then her response more likely will be silence or confusion. In such cases, teachers have to settle for ambiguity about what their students have learned during the reading conference, and it can be unnerving. Helping a student read the word *organism* is doable, and both teacher and student leave guided reading feeling like they have accomplished something. Asking questions that force students to probe more deeply into the text may not feel so immediately doable, and the interaction can feel, at times, less than successful. The following interaction, which continues the discussion of bacteria above, illustrates that point.

> STUDENT: Well, I guess there still are bad bacteria, so even though some are good, people like to use antibacterial soap because of the bad ones?
>
> TEACHER: Yes, I do think that's true. I'd like you to keep reading to yourself. Maybe you'll get more insights into this topic after you read some more. As you read, it's important to keep thinking about how what you read fits in with your knowledge of the world. That can seem hard, but the more you practice, the easier it will get.

The teacher and student both leave this interaction unsure of what they've accomplished. Teachers must maintain faith that over time and with prompting for deep meaning, students will begin to think more analytically about the texts they read.

TO SUMMARIZE

We have made the point in this chapter that individual conversations with students during guided reading are prime opportunities to ratchet up the demands that we make of them as readers. Teachers may have difficulty distinguishing between these levels, particularly between Levels 5 and 6. Much more important than figuring out which precise level any interaction represents is the commitment to present questions that require the cognitive demands represented by the right side of the continuum. Teachers should be mindful that stretching students in this way will not result in immediate changes in students' capacity for complex thinking about texts. Particularly when students are used to Level 1 to 3 demands, they may initially be unnerved by more challenging questions. In such cases, teachers should build up to the most challenging questions, starting first with Level 4, cumulative comprehension, before they move to Levels 5 and 6.

Chapters 7–9 are devoted to helping teachers make space for the kinds of interactions detailed in this chapter. Chapter 7 demonstrates where guided reading fits in with other aspects of literacy instruction, ensuring that teachers are able to make time for it in their already busy instructional days. Chapter 8 focuses on a structure for guided reading that privileges stretch conferences. Finally, by highlighting many examples of stretch conferences, Chapter 9 is designed to provide teachers with the understanding and tools that will increase their confidence and competence when prompting their students to deeper comprehension.

Part II

WRITING WORKSHOP DEFINED

Donald Graves (1983) was among the first to isolate the stages of writing and give them names. Along with that of his student, Lucy Calkins, Graves's work transformed writing instruction with its emphasis on process as well as product, student agency, authenticity of writing tasks, and collaboration. Educators ranging from kindergarten teachers to university professors have embraced this model of the writing process and created classroom practices to support student engagement in it. Though teachers instantiate the principles of writing workshop in many different ways, there are common characteristics, which include a focus on the stages of the writing process and on the social aspects of writing. In workshops, students learn about the process of writing from the teacher and from one another in a mutually supportive environment.

The process of revision receives much emphasis in writing workshop classrooms. Students are taught to work with their drafts as starting points, but then to literally re-see or re-vision their own ideas through interactions with peers and their teachers.

Because writing is prominent in standardized assessments designed to align with new standards, teachers may feel pressure to forgo writing workshop for more formulaic models of instruction. Research (i.e., Graham & Perin, 2006) suggests that students who receive writing instruction that emphasizes drafting, feedback, and revision, and gives students time and space to practice these parts of the process, do succeed on standardized tests of writing, in addition to possessing a more positive attitude toward writing.

Chapter 4 explains instructional elements central to writing workshop. Teachers who feel confident in their writing workshop instruction may wish to skip this discussion and go directly to Chapter 5 for a detailed discussion of writing conferences, the focus of this book. Chapter 6 offers many examples of high-quality writing conferences.

Making a Space for Conferences in a Writing-Rich Classroom

Teachers who privilege writing conferences do so in the context of a full complement of other instructional practices. This chapter introduces the instructional elements in writing workshop in order to demonstrate the location and specific function of writing conferences.

Students in writing workshop classrooms engage in the writing process, an idea forwarded by Donald Graves (1994) and taken up by many scholars and teachers since (see, for example, Atwell, 2014; Calkins, 1994; Cramer, 2001; Elbow, 1973, 1981; Fletcher & Portalupi, 2001; Graves, 1983). A teacher committed to writing workshop helps her students to function as adult writers might. Thus, as legitimate writers, students come up with ideas, plan those ideas, draft, get feedback, revise, and polish. A thorough discussion of classroom practices to support all aspects of writing workshop is beyond the bounds of this discussion. Please refer to the work of Ray (2004), Ray and Laminack (2001), Atwell (2014), Fletcher (2013), Fletcher and Portalupi (2001), Calkins (1994, 2006) for help with this. However, an overview that orients teachers to the role of conferences relative to other aspects of writing instruction may be helpful.

These components include:

1. Writing minilessons
2. Independent (journal) writing
3. Peer feedback
4. Instruction in grammar and mechanics

Each is described briefly below and, together with one-on-one writing conferences, comprise a classroom poised for supporting students as they develop as writers.

WRITING MINILESSONS

Students can benefit greatly from whole-group instruction in writing. Teachers should not hesitate to offer some instruction to students all at once, as long as this instruction is balanced with small-group and individual instruction, as it will be in a writing workshop classroom. Although minilessons have many different characteristics, the common denominator is that they are brief and focused upon a beneficial writing strategy. We elect to discuss two kinds of minilessons in particular, as these are among the most effective. Teachers often plan these lessons because they notice a trend when they conference with students individually. These trends become the data by which they determine the content of their minilessons. This process is explained in more detail below.

Minilessons in which teachers model their own writing process are important because they provide opportunities for students to witness a more experienced writer create meaning. In such lessons, the teacher uses a smart board, computer projected on a screen, flip chart, or whiteboard to compose (or plan or revise) as students watch. Students note this authentic experience of writing, which gives them a model from which to draw as they engage in their own writing. The teacher can demonstrate a particular strategy that she wishes to introduce to students, show a general writing session, or think through a writing problem as the students observe. The process by which this is done is analogous to a shared reading lesson (one is discussed in depth in Chapter 7) and includes the elements (and explications of those elements) that follow:

Launch: In a brief introduction, the teacher reminds students that she will be writing in front of them not as a teacher but as an actual writer. Thus, students will need to only watch and listen. As the teacher writes, she will not interact with the students, but rather try to authentically engage in her craft.

Modeling: The teacher writes (as mentioned before, in a way that all the students can view it) and as she is writing, thinks aloud. The students hear the teacher as she thinks through the choices she is making as a writer. The demonstration is brief, lasting only about 3 minutes.

Noticing: The teacher asks the students what they noticed that she did when she was writing. Student answers are collected and, sometimes, noted on the board or a chart, and discussed. The teacher may reinforce something she did while writing even if the students do not note it. This conversation may last up to 3 minutes.

Guided Practice: The students approximate the teacher's strategy in their journals as they practice what they just saw executed.

This process repeats often throughout the year, with different kinds of writing, different strategies, and different foci.

Below is an example of a teacher as she shares writing with her students in a minilesson:

TEACHER: Remember that when I am a writer, I cannot be a teacher. When I begin my writing, I am going to act as if I am alone in a room. I probably will talk to myself, but I am not talking to you. Just sit quietly and watch and listen. When I am done, I will ask you what you noticed I did when I was a writer.

Turns to write on whiteboard and stands for a minute with marker in hand.

Hmm, I think I am going to write about something that happened to me as I drove to school this morning. There were dozens and dozens of orange cones on this road and the traffic was backed up an unbelievable amount. When I got to the part where the construction should have been happening, the workers were all lying on the ground smoking and eating. Now, I understand that everyone needs a break, but this seemed so disrespectful given that we all were so inconvenienced. So I am going to start writing about that. Okay, here I go.

Turns to board and begins to write. Writes for a few minutes, narrating what she is doing. Turns back toward the students.

So what did you notice I did when I was a writer?

She collects a few answers, adding them to a list that she began early in the year. She then asks the students to pull out their journals and write about something that they have seen that aggravated them, trying out one of the strategies they saw her use.

Other times, teachers elect to use mentor texts to introduce or reinforce a concept that will have value for student writers. In this type of minilesson, the teacher selects a high-quality text that exemplifies a particular aspect of writing. After introducing it to the students as a read-aloud, or after they read the text themselves, the teacher leads a brief discussion about how this technique might be translated into their own writing. At times, the teacher may guide practice, having students attempt the strategy in a low-risk, nonassessed environment. There are many excellent books on selecting mentor texts that support various components of writing. (Please see, for example, Scholastic Books' series of Mentor Texts that accompany their Traits Writing series. These books suggest mentor texts for grade bands from kindergarten through 8th grade and can be used with or without the adoption of 6 +1 Traits.)

These are but two among many models of minilessons. Other models are effective as well, as long as they share the most important elements of a writing minilesson: They should be brief, repeated (anything worth doing once is worth reinforcing often), and tied directly to the needs of the writers in the classroom.

INDEPENDENT (JOURNAL) WRITING

Writers write to communicate to others and, sometimes, just for themselves. All developing writers should have the opportunity to use writing for a variety of purposes, including self-reflection, and a writing classroom can provide that opportunity. Independent, self-selected, nonassessed writing (some refer to this as journal writing) is an essential component of a writing workshop because it is authentic, and because it builds fluency and promotes a positive attitude toward writing. Every student should be given a short time, most days, to write about whatever they choose. Many teachers offer a large number of prompts that students can draw from at any time, and some students prefer this. Other students use writing to examine ideas, to narrate events, or to work out struggles. Teachers often ask how they can be certain that students are writing during independent writing time given that they don't read their entries. Many models for attending to this exist. Some teachers quickly glance at a number of journals just to be sure there is a quantity of writing there; others choose one or two at random and look more carefully. Still others circulate occasionally and look over the shoulder of a student or two who may be inclined toward off-task behavior. Whatever a teacher decides, it is most important to give students ownership over their writing during this time and to avoid spending too much time worrying about reading it. Many a writing teacher has heeded the warning that if you are reading everything students are writing, they aren't writing enough. As difficult as it is to give up the control that grading work affords, teachers must do it.

Independent writing is also important because it serves as a management tool in literacy classrooms in the following way. In order for writing workshop to function, students must be able to self-manage. Because there will be times when students are waiting for their opportunity to conference with the teacher, or when they have finished one element of the writing process while others have not, journal writing is an independent literacy activity that they can engage in while they wait. As it is effective in prompting growth in writing (and is often pleasurable), it is a great use of time.

In order to prepare students to use independent writing as a productive self-managed activity, teachers will need to set out expectations and practice building stamina for sustained concentration on independent writing. While some students have no problem writing for long stretches of time, others need to build up their abilities to concentrate on independent writing for increasingly longer periods. This process of building stamina is one that teachers use for independent reading as well. It has been our experience that students can, with practice, write steadily for longer and longer stretches as they go through a school year and as they progress through the grades. While 10 minutes is probably the maximum for early elementary students, upper elementary and middle grade writers may be able to work productively for 20 to 30 minutes given clear expectations and appropriate buildup.

PEER FEEDBACK

It is our practice to have students respond to one another's drafts before they get feedback from their teacher. We recommend setting up opportunities to peer conference, in pairs or in small groups, on the students' first drafts. Asking peers to be first readers develops the classroom community and gives student writers access to a legitimate, nonteacher audience. As we have been helping kids work effectively to respond to one another's writing for many years, we know that this interaction is powerful even if it is limited in its effect on the actual writing. As students often have strong reactions to writing but aren't quite sure why, it can be a challenge to translate student feedback into actual changes in writing. Nonetheless, social skills theorists (see Argyle, 1976, for example) argue that the similar cognitive constructs held by peers promote confidence, social skills, and motivation. Research has been spotty, however, on whether this interaction promotes writing achievement. We encourage teachers to develop a model for peer response that plays into students' comfort zones. Some teachers provide significant structure; others more loosely define the task. In any event, we encourage teachers to keep at these groups or pairs, to appreciate them for what they do contribute to student growth, and to keep expectations for them modest.

In Chapter 2, we introduced the Continuum of Task Complexity During Writing Conferences. Readers may recall that we suggested that teachers avoid Levels 1 (grammar and mechanics), 2 (word choice), and 3 (adding or taking away detail) when they conference individually with students. While we believe that grammar and mechanics are better focused upon later in the writing process, word choice and adding or omitting details are ideal elements for students to examine as they interact with one another around writing. As we noted in that earlier chapter, these are generally minor changes, but they can very much improve a student paper. In addition, they are within the reach of peers to notice and communicate.

We like to group students heterogeneously when they work in peer groups, as a great variety of perspectives is most useful when one is reading a draft to peers. Even weaker writers have the ability to say to stronger writers: "I think you could use more detail in this section," or, "I am not sure that this passage makes sense." Thus, these foci are appropriate as feedback in a peer-to-peer setting.

Even knowing that these kind of responses are well within student ability, teachers still must carefully prepare students to read clearly (their own papers), listen actively (to the papers of others), and respond kindly and thoughtfully to the writer.

INSTRUCTION IN GRAMMAR AND MECHANICS

We probably get no other question more commonly than "What is the role of correctness in writing workshop?" It is an absolute (but prevalent) misconception that writing workshop devalues grammar and mechanics. What it does do is contain it so that it isn't always the go-to first response from teachers and peers. Containing it means limiting conversation about it until the student has completed much of the content work, that is, has finished drafting and has received and used feedback about content from peers and the teacher. Once opportunities for content feedback (content being all that is not grammar or mechanics) have been provided and students have used the feedback to create revisions, attention must turn to the manner in which the paper is presented. This includes locating and correcting errors in Standard Written English, reconsidering sentence structures, examining spelling, and formatting the paper to the class specifications. Teachers manage this stage of the writing process in many ways. Often, teachers present minilessons on grammar and mechanics, distinct from those minilessons focused upon content as described above, in response to errors that they note a variety of students are demonstrating in their written work. The topics covered in those minilessons (e.g., punctuation, sentence boundaries, spelling rules, subject/verb agreement) are noted carefully as students prepare their papers for submission. Far from devaluing the role of grammar and mechanics in proficient student writing, writing workshop proponents have placed these elements of writing in a particular stage of the writing process. In addition, they have heeded the research (i.e., Smith, Cheville, & Hillocks, 2006) indicating that grammar and mechanics are best taught and practiced in the context of student writing rather than on practice sheets or prewritten texts that students did not create on their own.

A WORD ABOUT MANAGEMENT

Because making space for one-on-one writing conferences requires teachers to focus on just one student at a time, preparation for self-regulation on the part of the other students is essential. In order to maintain successful management and productivity, students need to be taught that once they are through with their first draft, they place their name on a waiting list and go directly to their journals, where they are to write for the maximum amount of time possible, or until a peer group is formed, or until the teacher calls them for their turn, or until the workshop is over. While we say this so casually, "Students need to be taught" it isn't casual at all. Teachers who have had the most success with conferences have done so in large part because the rest of the students know what to do when they are in a transitional period. Management includes attention to the following details and understandings that students must have as a prerequisite to beginning one-to-one conferences:

1. Students know where their journals are housed.
2. Students know where to put their names or otherwise indicate that they have completed one aspect of the writing process and are ready for the next.
3. Students can locate writing utensils that are functional.
4. Students have shown that they can write productively for a significant stretch of time.

For some teachers, these steps may seem unnecessary, but our experience has taught us that even the smallest hiccup (like a student being unable to locate a tablet, pencil, or his journal) can cause a break in the teacher's concentration on the student with whom she is working in a conference. We urge teachers to practice these processes during the 1st month of school when routines are being set. Refer to the work of Boushey and Moser on the Daily

Five (2014) and CAFÉ (2009) models of literacy learning for sensible ways to help students learn these routines. It is also worthy of note that similar processes must be in place for success in guided reading (as discussed in Chapter 7), so some of this work does serve double duty in preparing students for both. Teachers are not likely to have success during writing conferences if they cannot give each student the kind of attention needed, the kind of attention that is not available if one eye is always on the rest of the class. Once this management is in place, conferences can begin. The next chapter talks very specifically about how to run conferences that focus on complex ideas in student writing.

CHAPTER 5

Structuring Writing Conferences

This question plagues teachers and can make the idea of incorporating writing conferences daunting. In Chapter 2, we discussed using the Continuum of Task Complexity During Writing Conferences to prompt high-quality interactions with students about their writing. In presenting those examples, we excerpted the relevant portions of the conference. This chapter presents a complete conference model that includes greeting the students and sending them off to do their work. As time commitment is so often a barrier, this chapter suggests ways for teachers to manage conferences so they don't become unwieldy. At the completion of this chapter, teachers will have a specific model for talking to students in writing conferences. Even with a solid model, however, writing conferences can present numerous challenges. In order to encourage teachers to give conferences a fair shot, we start with three suggestions:

1. As indicated in Chapter 4, the remainder of the class must be functioning without teacher direction in order for writing workshop to succeed. Until the teacher is confident that this can happen, conferences should not begin.
2. Each conference should be under 5 minutes and, because this time goes so quickly, should be tightly structured and consistent from student to student and paper to paper. This helps both with teacher time management and with student understanding, as the student gets used to the manner in which the conferences flow and the teacher is able to hasten the conversation. Though 5 minutes is brief, teachers find that with practice, it is, in fact, the right amount of time.
3. If, because of large class size or an inability of the teacher to speak and think quickly enough, individual conferences with

the whole class are untenable, consider this hybrid model: For the first paper, the teacher meets with half of the students and takes the second set of student papers home to respond. For the second paper, the teacher switches and meets with the other half. This way, students will get conferences on every other paper, which is not ideal, but often much more manageable for the teacher.

EFFECTIVE CONFERENCES

This model began as a scaffold for teachers just beginning to do writing conferences. We expected that once they became confident and proficient, they would not use it any longer. However, while we do see that experienced teachers treat the conference more flexibly, they share that the structure is useful even as they gain confidence. It helps them keep to the time allotment, in addition to helping students know how to listen. If teachers are surprised by the brevity that we suggest, we aren't surprised to hear it. Many teachers are startled by just how much they can communicate in such a short time. Even so, teachers new to conferences will have to be more generous with the time allotments. As teachers gain experience, the conferences will go much faster. The times listed in Figure 5.1 below should serve only as a guide; teachers shouldn't feel they must conform to them in lockstep. It is simply that the more quickly each conference goes, the more conferences teachers can do. Teachers need to remember, however, that as they begin holding conferences, and even for the whole 1st year, they are really working on their own skills in a new kind of instruction that has both management and cognitive challenges. It is worth it, but it is certainly an initial adjustment. If a teacher only gets to 10 of 30 students during the first paper, he should plan to get to the next 10 during the next paper and the final 10 during the third. Though students surely need feedback from their teacher on most writing assignments, it doesn't always have to be in the form of a conference. Less ideal, but still helpful, are written responses that contain the same elements that the conferences contain. We hope to move much of the work of the teaching of writing into the classroom

Figure 5.1. Elements of a Writing Conference

Timing goal	Student role	Teacher role
90 seconds	Student reads paper	Listens
30 seconds	Listens	Responds as a person
30 seconds	Listens and thinks	Thinks aloud
60 seconds	Listens and thinks	Responds as a writing teacher with Levels 4a, 4b, or 5 prompts
90 seconds	Says back what is heard	Writes down what the student says on a Post-it

rather than having teachers read student papers when they are at home, without the student present. In the transition, however, teachers may do some of both.

Figure 5.1 provides an example that includes all of the important elements of a writing conference. Following presentation of the model, each part is explained separately. This model originated in work with secondary students. For a fuller discussion of it, please see Berne, 2008.

It is important to reiterate, prior to discussion of the above figure, that the point of conferences is not to "fix" the paper at hand. Instead, it is to teach the writer something about writing, something that may or may not show up in the next draft of this paper. In Chapter 1, we introduced the idea that we can often simplify reading and writing by offering feedback that is benign. We sometimes refer to this practice as *teaching around* complexity. For teachers of student writers, there are always small things to mention that could improve a paper (and these are noted as part of the left side of the continuum). We also suggested in Chapter 4 that adding a detail and using describing words are both elements that can be attended to through peer feedback or discussed in whole-group contexts. Teachers should use the short time they have to work individually with students on their writing to teach a concept, not to show students where to do something specific. Conferences are not necessarily tied to a more successful future draft, but, rather, to a more successful future writer.

The conference, thus, is organized so that students get a big idea to take away from it, ponder, and then try. Teachers who use stretch conferences understand and reflect in their assessment that the skill or strategy that is introduced in the conference is a developing skill or strategy, and may not show up fully formed in this paper.

During the weeks that teachers prepare students to function independently in writing workshop (i.e., helping them build stamina for independent writing, teaching them the logistics involved in self-management, helping them learn to listen to their peers read), the teacher can take some time to show videos of conferences done in previous years, share transcripts of past conferences, and present to students the elements that a conference entails. This preparation will help make the actual conferences run more smoothly, as the purpose for each element will have been explicated prior to the student-teacher meetings.

UNPACKING THE CONFERENCE

The student reads the paper. The first element of the conference is student reading. Though some teachers find it easier to concentrate on the paper if they read it themselves, it is important to hear the paper in the author's voice. Young authors often attend to their own writing as they read aloud in a way that they do not when reading silently. Time and again, students will stop themselves mid-paper to note, "That isn't really what I meant there," or "Maybe I should explain that a little more." When this occurs, the writer should be encouraged to make a quick notation as she reads, but then move on. The teacher also might make a note of it. Similarly, the teacher may hear a voice, a tone, or a pace that will help him to see where this paper might go. That said, teachers often look over the student's paper as they read, both listening and tracking the text themselves. A teacher who absolutely cannot respond from just an oral read will have to adjust this structure to work for her. Teachers sometimes wonder if they should listen to the whole paper if it is lengthy. Our experience is that anything up to 3 pages can be read in the context of a brief conference. Teachers should encourage students not to write much more than this, as it is easier to teach and learn with shorter pieces. If a student can sustain a topic for longer, however, the teacher might have to preview the text and only have the student read a portion. It is difficult to respond only to portions of a paper, as invariably the young author assures the teacher that what they recommended comes later in the paper. Only a very few students are apt to write far more than is manageable in a short interaction, though.

The teacher responds as a person. Once the student has completed his or her reading, the teacher begins the feedback portion of the conference. One of the challenges for teachers is to put away their teacher hat and put on their reader hat. It is very important for a writer to understand that the writing communicates something from one person to another, and that it is not merely an assignment to complete. To do this in the most authentic way, teachers might think about how a piece of writing affects them as a reader, not just how to teach students something about it. Thus, the first portion of feedback is a gut response. We call this "responding as a person" in recognition that teachers often forgo this important response component and rush to teach. Some examples of this first response are listed below:

- I had no idea your family takes this kind of driving vacation every year. I always wanted to do that when I was a kid, but my parents always wanted to stay close to home.
- This is such a funny story to me because I can actually see you crashing your bike into that pile of leaves.
- How sad that your grandmother passed, but how wonderful that she was so special to you.

As these examples illustrate, there is no wrong response. Again, the difficulty for teachers, often, is turning off their teacher ear and turning on their reader ear. Students should also be taught, as they prepare for individual conferences with their teachers, that this response need not prompt any changes in their writing. Students often don't have a great arsenal of experiences in which teachers look at their academic work and respond in such a way that there is no requirement to do anything about it, so they may wonder what action they should take in response to all comments. That this initial comment is merely a part of sharing a real response is a lesson that can be taught and is usually understood after the first conference or so.

The teacher thinks aloud. Following the initial response to the piece of writing, teachers often take a moment to gather their thoughts as they prepare to give the kind of complex feedback necessary in a writing conference. If teachers do this while thinking aloud, they provide a unique opportunity for students to glimpse into the mind of a more expert reader as he considers how to respond to a paper. This component of the conference may be a bit messy as teachers talk through their response, perhaps rejecting one idea, perhaps weighing the benefit of one piece of feedback over another. Teachers shouldn't be concerned about whether students are following this word for word. Rather, the purpose is to model for students how the feedback they will receive developed. Examples of the kind of thinking a teacher might do as the student listens are:

- I wonder if there is a way for Joey to tell me this so that I know it is an argument. As it is, it sounds like he really isn't convinced, so I am not sure.
- This is an incredible paper and I am so very moved by it. I wonder what I can tell Alicia that will be of value.
- I know exactly what I want to say because I'll bet Kyle doesn't know how much I want to hear precisely how his family functions. This will be so much more powerful if it is tied to his specific circumstances.

Teachers often find this portion of the conference a little awkward. It isn't always comfortable to let a student hear a teacher in mid-thought, so some teachers omit this conference element. The conference still functions without it, but the opportunity it affords will be missed. Sometimes the next portion, in which the student receives direct feedback from the teacher, is a partial repeat, in clearer language, of the think-aloud. Such an occurrence is fine, as the writing teacher now translates his thinking into feedback that the student will use to revise the paper. Sometimes this means the student hears the feedback more than once (which is also fine). Other times the student notes that the teacher thought one thing about her paper, yet decided to go another way with the feedback. This is valuable as well.

The teacher responds as a writing teacher (using the continuum). The next component of the conference is what distinguishes a stretch conference. This book argues that a one-on-one interaction is the ideal place to push kids to think through literacy processes that may be nascent, developing, or not yet understood. The final component of the writing conference, offering feedback, is where this push happens. The feedback is designed, as readers will recall from Chapter 2, not as a way to "fix" a particular paper, but as a way to use student work to incite thinking about writing in total. Inviting students to do something that may not result in a better paper is a bold move for teachers, yet it is the essence of teaching the writer. The other difficulty in this portion of the stretch conference is knowing what feedback is appropriately challenging and developmentally in sync with student needs.

In order to make decisions about what feedback to provide, a teacher might reflect upon what actually would make this piece of writing more engaging. Teachers don't often consider student writing in the same way they would consider writing produced by anyone else. This model is designed to push the complexity of in-school writing to the level of authentic writing. The continuum explained in Chapter 2 supports this important work of pushing our responses in order to elevate expectations, expand the notion of what good student writing is, and better align it with just plain good writing. A 4th-grader may never produce a piece of writing that satisfies the sophistication of an adult reader, yet even young writers have ideas and stories that are worthy of a read if given the opportunity to share with someone who responds as a reader. An excerpt from this kind of feedback appears below. As it is difficult to capture the complexity of feedback of this sort without context, the entire paper is included. For this example, only part three, the stretch comment, is provided. The section following is a transcript of a full conference with another student.

This paper is written by a 5th-grader:

My Trip to the River:

This story happened a few years ago, when I was smaller. It was a cold day, so my mom bundled up my brother and I. That was usual. My family (including me), and some of my mom's friends went on a trip to the river. I can't remember what my mom's friends name's were. Malcolm, my brother, was bored, so he decided to pick on me. You know how brothers are. We road in a boat. It was my first time riding in a boat. I didn't get to ride in boat's that often. Malcolm was teasing me about the boat tipping. Then, my mom dropped the paddle. She got it back though. We ate, and then headed on up the trail that led to the truck. Malcolm reached out for my hat and missed. It fell in the river. He reached out to pick it up as it started to drift away. He reached a little further. Malcolm got ahold of it. Splash! He fell in. My brother started to panic. Help I'm drowning! he said. Everyone just stood there. One of my mom's friends told him to stand up if he wanted to live. He found out the water was only up to his knees. I laughed. He didn't think it was funny!

Teacher stretch comment:

I think the interesting part of this, for me, is that your brother was really nasty to you, then he was put at risk by falling in the water and you seemed cold about that. I would like you to think about what this story is saying about the relationship of you and your brother. There is a lot going on here related to teasing and probably feelings of both frustration and worry. I want you to think about how you can bring that interesting part of the paper to a more prominent part of the piece. Instead of dropping me into the center of the story, I feel like there needs to be some kind of setup or beginning that orients me to the feelings involved. Otherwise, I just read it as a story of "something that happened." I need to understand why this was an important representation of your relationship with your brother, if it was.

Clearly what the teacher is asking of this student goes beyond the simple insertion of a feeling or two. She is working at a high level of complexity by asking for a purpose (Level 5 on the continuum) and a reorganization around that purpose (Level 4b on the continuum). It may very well be that the student is only able to respond to her feedback in a simplistic way. However, such a response does not automatically deem the conference an unsuccessful interaction. The teacher is building knowledge for the student of what good writing can do: namely, take a small story and allow the reader to generalize a greater idea from it. She is simultaneously teaching him that writers don't often present stories without context. This particular writer may not be able to understand these ideas fully yet, but to be the writer that he can be, he needs to start working on that notion. His teacher will remind him of this as he continues writing through the school year and as the months go on, with support from whole-group instruction, will expect to see development of a framing purpose in this student's writing. The next chapter will contain many more versions of this portion of the conference.

The student says back what is heard. The final portion of the conference is devoted to the student's reiteration of the teacher's comments. The teacher asks the student, "What did you hear me say?" or prompts the student to "Repeat my comments," in order to clarify for herself and the student what their understandings are. Teachers often jot the reiteration down on a Post-it so the student has a record of what was said. For younger students, teachers sometimes record the whole conference and have the student play it back before beginning to work on the paper again. Often, teachers wish to have a record for themselves of what was said in the conference, and can acquire that by jotting down a quick note as the next student transitions into the conference. However it is managed, we see value in having the student:

1. Listen to the feedback
2. Repeat the feedback
3. Walk away with the main points of the feedback

The Post-it also can act as a memory jog for the teacher as she reviews the final draft, following completion of the writing project. Chapter 8, on guided reading conferences, provides many more ideas about record-keeping. The same ideas will be effective for writing conferences.

A SAMPLE CONFERENCE

The structure this model provides helps students and teachers, as it alerts them to what to expect from the interaction. Students know that the first piece of feedback, responding as a person, will not require a response from them. They also know that the next utterance, *thinking aloud*, will be the teacher working out her own thinking as she prepares to give feedback, and that this portion may make sense or it may be a bit rambling. The final comment, *responding as a writing teacher*, will be the one in which the teacher will attempt to teach the student something about writing. The students will listen to the feedback knowing that they will be expected to attempt the teacher's recommendation, but that they won't be expected to master anything. They also understand that they will be asked to repeat back what they have heard and then return to their desks to work with the feedback. Many teachers keep the structure jotted down and handy as they are starting to hold conferences because they find that it keeps them on task and attentive to their time constraints. Below is the complete transcript of a conference re-created from observation notes. The various elements of the conference structure are indicated and separated by section for easy identification. This 6th-grade student's paper, provided prior to the transcript of the conference, is a response to an assignment to argue something about which he is passionate. In the actual conference, the student would first read the paper to his teacher.

Medical research involving animals has dramatically improved the health of the human race. Without animal testing, the cure for polio would not exist and diabetics would suffer or die from their disease. Despite these benefits, some people believe that animals should be not be used for testing medical techniques and drugs. This essay will outline the advantages of animal testing.

Animal testing allows scientists to test and create new drugs. Animals such as monkeys or rabbits have similar physical processes to humans. This allows scientists to test the effects of certain drugs. If a drug produces adverse effects in animals, it is probably unfit for human use.

Animal testing is cheap. There is a large supply of animals for medical research. Animals are easily bred and maintained safely in controlled labs. The costs of testing on humans would be extremely high.

Many people argue that animal testing is cruel. In some cases, this is true. However, it would be much more cruel to test new drugs on people or children, or to let people die because there was not enough information about a drug. Furthermore, legislation in most countries sets standards for animal treatment, and laboratories have guidelines to prevent cruelty.

Opponents of animal research also say that information from animals does not apply to humans. They point to certain commercial drugs, which have been withdrawn because of side effects in humans. While it is true that animal systems differ from human systems, there are enough similarities to apply information from animals to humans.

Animal rights campaigners claim that we don't need new tests because we already have vast amounts of information. However, many new deadly infections appear every year and new treatments and drugs are needed to combat these deadly plagues.

Animal testing is needed in the world we live in. Our responsibility is to manage the animals in our care and balance their suffering against the good that comes from them.

Teacher:

(Responding as a person) This makes me think of my grandmother who died way too early because they had not come up with a way to detect the cancer she had early enough. I always wondered if they did more testing sooner, if she would have lived.

(Thinking aloud) This is an interesting topic, but my goodness I have heard so many students write about this very thing over the years. I wonder if Jonathan can distinguish his argument from all the other arguments I have heard. I might be able to draw on a whole-class lesson we did, so I am going to try.

(Responding as a writing teacher) I wonder if you can tell me more about why you chose this as your topic. I see that you have a lot of information here, but it feels a little like you are just ticking off facts. Even in a formal paper like this one, you want your reader to be right with you and believe in what you say. If I put all the papers down in the middle of the room and they had no names, do you think I would know this was yours? I want you to think about how really good writers sound like they are speaking in their own voice even when they are writing on serious subjects such as this one. You have shown me that you can organize arguments and keep on topic and that is great. Now I want you to try to be you when you do so. Remember when I modeled my own writing and it sounded so flat, remember that I tried to make it sound like my own speaking? Remember that I decided that if I couldn't say something unique about it that I might as well not say anything at all, and so I referred to more personal examples? Those are three things you can think about to see if you can put your signature on it. Now, can you say back what you heard me say?

STUDENT (Student repeats feedback): You said that I should be more convincing and you wanted me to tell you more about that and you wanted me to make it sound more like me, and can you remind me what the three ways are?
TEACHER: I have just jotted them down on this sticky note for you so you can refer to them later. I am really looking forward to seeing the work you put into your revision.

In this conference with a reasonably strong student writer, the teacher acknowledges what this student already knows how to do: organize a paper, stay on topic, and present ideas with clarity. She uses most of the conference, therefore, to instruct the student on what is not represented in the paper. It may be that the student would have to undo some of the tight structure of this argument in order to accomplish what the teacher asks, and he may not be ready to do so. However, his teacher sees that he can already write in one kind of way and wants him to stretch to see what else he can do in this genre. At the least, she sets him up to develop a notion of what a reader needs to engage with the paper fully.

FORMATIVE ASSESSMENT DURING WRITING CONFERENCES

One immeasurable benefit of listening to student writing during conferences is the ability to use the data to plan future instruction. When teachers look across a group of student conferences, they can get a sense of where the class is as a whole. Even if the feedback the teacher gives varies wildly, there may be common aspects to the students' writing that she notes, but does not attend to in the one-on-one environment. For example, a teacher may notice that students are making claims in their writing without offering counterclaims. While this is certainly important, it is contextual and tied, likely, to a specific assignment. It also is readily taught to a whole group. The lesson is likely pertinent to a whole range of writers: Those who are strong may have strong unchallenged arguments; those writers who are weak may have weak unchallenged arguments. Both can be taught through a minilesson like those discussed in Chapter 4, and that lesson can be applied to this paper or future papers. Instead of attending to the need for counterclaims during the conference, something that might distract the students from tangling with less specific issues, the teacher plans a series of minilessons. Far from devaluing this aspect of writing, the teacher attends to it carefully. She just does it at another point in her writing instruction.

In the next chapter, we revisit the tenets of the Continuum of Task Complexity During Writing Conferences and offer many more examples of the ways that teachers use the continuum to prompt growth in student writers.

CHAPTER 6

Students and Teachers Conference About Writing

In order to continue examining the way in which the writing continuum scaffolds rich conferences, in this chapter we will present a number of student/teacher conferences. The student papers are in their original form, without any supplemental editing. Procedurally, it is helpful to note that during each of these conferences, the student read the paper aloud to the teacher, who listened in addition, in most cases, to following along by looking at the paper as it was read. For the sake of time and space, after the first conference, only the most relevant excerpts from the interaction are presented. Following each one is an annotation that helps to explain our perspective on the conference.

The teachers involved in the conferences presented in this chapter had significant experience with conferences as part of their regular instruction in writing. We have elected to present conferences that we view as very-high-quality in order to offer some models for consideration. Many of the conferences follow the precise format presented in Chapter 5 (recalling that the teacher responds as a person, shares her thinking, responds as a writing teacher, and asks the student to summarize the feedback); others vary this structure a bit.

The papers represented in these conferences cross genres, but are largely focused upon the three genres in current vogue with schools, due, in part, to their prominence in the new Common Core State Standards for Writing: narrative writing, argumentative writing, and expository writing. Some student compositions draw on outside sources or were prompted by a reading. Others were written in response to a prompt that was not linked to other texts or was chosen independently by the student author. Student authors range from 4th to 8th grade and are from a variety of urban, rural, and suburban school districts.

Following each student paper, but before sharing the conference, a brief analysis of the paper is presented in a section called "Considering the Paper." This analysis sometimes foreshadows the content of the conference, but also may offer multiple considerations. The conferences usually focus on only one instructional component (as discussed before), though there may be numerous ideas to which the teacher might attend. In the "Considering the Paper" sections, we offer any number of complex ideas that a teacher might elect to share.

5TH-GRADE WRITER

The paper below, "My Life So Far," was written by a 5th-grade student late in the spring. Although the students had written many papers during the year, this was the first one where the teacher allowed students to select their own topic, without a prompt. The student chose to write about her feelings about her parents and others she feels have supported her life thus far:

> I have wonderful parents that give me lots of stuff to play with!!! I have a lot of friends that like me!! Eva loves me and is always there for me if I need help even though she is three. All the teachers and all my friends help me learn but it's not really easy things it is challenging things!!! My WONDERFUL parents and my FAVORITE sister love me very much. My mom and dad spent money so I could play the piano!!! My mom never gave up when she tried to have me and then she had Julia 3 year later. She was lucky because she was in the hospital 4 times before she had Julia and I!!!

Considering the paper. This paper has a lot of heart, but it is more akin to a journal entry than a finished piece of writing. Though it has many promising aspects, the author's intention in presenting it isn't entirely clear. In addition, although it is ostensibly about the author, much more focus is placed on the people and things that surround her. Below is a reproduction of the conference based upon fieldnotes.

TEACHER: First I want to say that I think your parents and sister will dearly love reading this. It is really nice to hear so many wonderful things about them. Okay, I am just going to look over this one more time so that I am sure I know what I want to say . . . um-hm, okay, I think I am ready. I want to ask you what you wanted me to know from reading this piece. And I am going to ask you to think about the answer before you tell me.

STUDENT: To tell you about my family and the good things in my life.

TEACHER: And I think you have done that, but I wonder if you could think about why I might want to know about your family. Instead of thinking about just you as the writer, could you think about me as the reader? What should I take away from this?

STUDENT: That I'm doing good because all these people love me.

TEACHER: Okay. I'm wondering, if someone I didn't know well came up to me and started telling me about their family, someone just started talking, I think I would wonder why they are telling me all this. What is a good reason for me to learn about your family?

STUDENT: Because . . .

TEACHER: I will tell you something. I actually am very interested in your family and that is because I know you. I would love to know how these characteristics of your family members have shaped you, or made you the way you are. I wonder if you might begin the paper by describing something about you and then reflect on the way that what you have seen in your family made you that way. Do you think you could start that?

STUDENT: Yes.

TEACHER: Can you say back to me what you heard me say?

STUDENT: I heard you say that you wanted me to add a part of my paper where I talk about myself and how I am like my family.

TEACHER: That is right. Start there and see where it goes.

In this conference, the teacher is aware that the student is writing without a clear understanding of her audience. In order to share this notion with the student, she talks with her about setting a purpose. This is a complex, Level 5 discussion because it focuses on the "why does this matter" question. While the student may not have a clear notion yet of how she might respond to the feedback from her teacher, at the very least she is gaining the idea that writers often make choices based upon an understanding of their readers' needs. This can be a very productive line of instruction, one that we know will take time, modeling, and practice, but ultimately results in much better writing.

7TH-GRADE WRITER

The paper below was written by a 7th-grader. The student was asked to write about something that he believed to be controversial, and he chose the use of animals in research on medical advances for humans.

> Animal testing has benefited human health. People do not contract polio anymore because of a vaccine tested on animals. Advances in antibiotics, insulin, and other drugs have been made possible through research done on animals. Animal testing should continue to benefit medical research.
>
> In order for scientists to create new drugs, they have to be able to test them. Scientists have found that many animals have similar physical processes to humans. Watching how a new drug affects an animal makes it possible to find out how new drugs might effect the human body.
>
> The cost of animal testing makes it an affordable option. Laboratory animals are in abundance. It is easy to get rats and other animals and to keep them in labs.
>
> Animal testing saves human lives. It would be wrong to test new drugs on humans. How many people would die because doctors could not administer medication before compiling all the information about a new drug? When surveyed, 99% of all active doctors in the United States stated that animal research has paved the way to many medical advancements. An impressive 97% of doctors support the continuous use of animals for research.

Animal testing should be continued for medical research. It provides a safe method for drug testing that is inexpensive and easy to maintain. Doctors endorse the usage of animals for testing. It is possible that the cure for AIDS could come about through animal testing.

Considering the paper. This student has many ideas, and many are defensible. However, it isn't clear where he is getting his information or exactly why he has put it together as he has. As it is, it is more like a list of reasons rather than a reasoned argument. In addition, there is not much that is unique to this student's writing. There isn't anything really compelling or interesting enough to hold a reader's attention.

TEACHER: I think you have a lot of good arguments, but I am not sure I follow how this argument is unique to you. I see where you state what you want to prove, that animal testing should continue, but I don't see separate reasons. And I don't see that your reasons are distinctly yours. Your reasons seem to kind of run together, more like you are chatting with me than you have distinct points, and those points don't seem to be points that I couldn't look up and find anywhere. That is the first thing I would like you to work on. Maybe start by drawing boxes and putting your reasons in them. This will help you to see if you indeed do have reasons that are strong and ordered logically.

STUDENT: Okay.

TEACHERS: And I think what that organizer will also do is help you to determine if you have an opposing view. I am not sure I see the other side of the argument and how you respond to it.

In the remainder of the conference, the teacher asks the student to start sketching out the graphic organizer. This is what she uses to be sure the student understood her directions. While the student had a lot to say, his ideas weren't distinct enough and that made them less compelling. We note that the demands of this reorganization are significant. The student may need additional support in order to be successful. His teacher will have taken note of that and, looking across student papers, may have designed some whole-group instruction in support of her comments. Once the teacher notes that this is a trend in the student writing she sees, she can teach directly toward that in a whole-group setting.

4TH-GRADE WRITER

This next student, a 4th-grader, is responding to a prompt from an informational text that discusses the natures of and differences between type 1 and type 2 diabetes. The teacher attends to her written response to a prompt that asked students to share what they learned about diabetes. The excerpt from this conference starts when the teacher begins a discussion of the organization of the response.

> In this text I learned how the doctors used to treat their patients. They did it the same way they do it today, but the doctors would use insulin from either a cows pancreas or a pigs pancreas. If anyone with type one Diabetes today would have been in big trouble before the 1920s. The first person to get this treatment was a 14 year old Canadian boy named Leonard Thompson. He lived another 13 years before he died. Now insulin is made in a lab and has saved the lives of a lot of people.

Considering the paper. This response to reading doesn't have any organizational coherence, and there isn't a sense of the student understanding the difference between summary, detail, argument, and main idea. If the teacher was using this writing to discern something about the student's comprehension of this text, she might infer that the student absorbed many of the facts but didn't show how they were related to one another in meaningful ways.

> TEACHER: Since you summarized the text really thoroughly, I can see that you understood it. I was very interested in what struck you from the text that you didn't know before. When presenting information like this, you want to be sure that you help the reader see what the relationship is between your

ideas. It is not enough to list the things you learned. Can you give us a sense of setup, maybe like an introduction first, then the details, then a conclusion? Otherwise, it is hard for me to know where this is going. Remember when we read that article in class that set up that boy's trip to the planetarium? Remember that before he told us what he saw he said what he was doing at the planetarium and after what his favorite part was? This isn't exactly like that, but it is the same concept. You already know some things about diabetes, so maybe your introduction can let your reader know that you have some knowledge already. Then, after discussing what you learned, maybe linking it together some, you could write another concluding paragraph about what of those things was the most interesting and why. Do you see how that mirrors the structure of the mentor text we looked at without copying it exactly?

This teacher has given the student plenty of feedback. As she listened to the student read, she noted that the student didn't set a context for the writing and then left the reader hanging at the end. She was able to draw from a previous whole-class minilesson where she had introduced a mentor text to her students and related that structure to the one she hopes the student will begin to design for this paper. The teacher has asked the student to do three major things: add a beginning, connect together the middle, and finish with a conclusion. This Level 4b feedback (organizing around a genre) is complicated for a young student and can be difficult. Maybe the student will do one of those things. Maybe she will try them all. In any event, there is a bigger lesson embedded in the comments. In addition, this teacher expertly draws on a large-group lesson and applies it to an individual student paper.

8TH-GRADE WRITER

Eighth-graders were asked to argue for something that is relevant to their lives. This student elected to recommend some changes in the materials acquisition of the school library.

My younger sister sits in the dentist's office paging through
People Magazine. Wow, she says, did you know that Brittany
Spears has had three husbands and that she has two children?
Is this information I want a youngster (she is 8) to have? I feel
that schools should not subscribe to popular magazines such as
this one.

I feel this way because sometimes the articles are mislead-
ing or inappropriate. Some students might not know the difference between right and wrong and this clearly won't help. I get
Seventeen magazine at home every month. There are some articles that I feel should not be allowed in a school. For example,
getting a boyfriend or losing weight.

These magazines have inappropriate content and kids get
enough of that on TV and on the internet. Even these things are
in school but they are controlled so that the really bad stuff isn't
allowed. Internet filters keep stuff out of the library and then
the stuff is just sitting their in magazines!

School libraries should be places to study seriously and get
materials for classes. Especially since funding is short, libraries
shouldn't spend their money on what is not part of the school
curriculum.

Considering the paper. While this student does a nice job beginning with something unique, her argument isn't coherent or especially effective because it wanders around. Though the thesis is
clear, some of the supports are in conflict with it.

This teacher first compliments the student on her personal anecdote and talks about how that drew her into the argument. She
then begins to note some inconsistencies in the paper that might be
considered in a revision:

TEACHER: Now that you have gotten me engaged in this text, you
have every opportunity to really convince me of your point
of view. However, I am not sure I understand if there is really
another side? Do you see these magazines in our library? And
is that okay because we are a junior high? Or is it not okay
at all? I am not sure what precisely you are saying because
you start off with your young sister and she isn't in a school
library and then you move to your own reading at home, then

you get to the part about schools not until the end of the second body paragraph. I am not sure that everything you say is really about these being at school libraries. You have an interesting argument, but I want to be sure that you aren't drifting off to other topics. I would like you to go through with a highlighter and mark the parts in the text that pertain only to these kinds of texts in schools. Also, can you be much clearer about whether you mean all libraries or just those in elementary schools? You seem to think these are okay for you to read, at least at home, so I am getting a little lost.

This teacher notes some inconsistencies in the student's writing. Rather than point this out explicitly, however, she uses this opportunity to talk to the student about an organizational structure (Level 4b) that supports argumentation. This may result in a new thesis (or not), but it certainly helps the student understand how coherence, an important part of organization, assists with an argument's power.

6TH-GRADE WRITER

A 6th-grader who struggles with writing produced the following text. This student has special needs and works in the regular language arts class with support from an instructional aide. The teacher and the aide have worked together to be sure that the aide talks with the student prior to writing to help set his ideas in motion, but that the student does the physical writing and the cognitive work independently. The teacher had concerns that in previous years, the student dictated to an aide who may have put her own spin on the ideas by altering what the student was actually saying. Though this may have been well intentioned, it (at least partially) masked the student as a writer. Without access to a student's actual abilities, instruction is easily mismatched to needs. A stretch conference is potent because the teacher uses the student writing as data to make decisions about this individualized instruction.

If I were rich I would use it to go to coledge. My parents would not have to worry about how I was going to go to coledge and they wouldn't have to work so hard to save. I want to go to coledge to be a lawer to decide who is right.

With all the money left over. I would give to poor people in my neighborhood. And for them I would shower them with money so there were no poor people left.

Some people would waste the money on cars of houses or candy or motrsikles. I would do good for me and family and everyone else if I were rich.

Considering the paper. This paper is unique, and it is wonderful to see that this writer has something in his life that he wishes to share. Sometimes struggling writers are more facile with ideas than more skillful ones because they don't have the fear of error, and are less conservative and more apt to just try something out. Now that the writer has his ideas on paper, he needs to figure out what he wants his audience to get out of the text. This may be a paper about poverty, about ambition, about selflessness—right now it isn't entirely clear. However, it is worth noting that it probably has more life than some papers written by students whose writing has always been categorized as better than his. Certainly many 6th-graders write with more precision and adhere more closely to the standards of English, but this student should be appreciated for what he brings to the table, too.

The teacher complimented him on the ideas he presented, noted that his ambitions are admirable, and then began presenting feedback. The student is in the company of his instructional aide as he sits with the teacher. The aide's role is to listen as well so that when the student returns to work on his revision, she can help the student recall the teacher's feedback.

> TEACHER: So, I see some real progress from you, and I think that is wonderful. In your next draft, I would like to get a much clearer sense of this paper as teaching us something about you. As it is, I feel like you are almost saying something about how different you are than others, but it isn't quite there. Or maybe I am missing the main point?
>
> STUDENT: I'm not sure.
>
> TEACHER: Let's think about one thing you could do that would make the purpose of this very clear.

STUDENT: I don't know.

TEACHER: What about if you talked some more about the idea that your ideas about how to use your money are so different from those of other people. You are right that many young people only think about their own material things, and that they aren't always generous about their families and their communities. What if you started with that idea and maybe told us how you know that to be true? Do you have an idea that you could start by presenting a conversation that you overheard or participated in where kids your age were talking about money and how it was very superficial or only about them wanting phones or clothes and then you started to think about your life and saw it differently? I wonder if just adding that element and putting it at the beginning might really help me to understand how and why you are so different from other kids. And I know that to be the case because I know you.

There is so much to work on in this text that it can become overwhelming for teacher and student. Often, teachers respond to this by suggesting that the student do many, many things. In turn, this confuses the student, who changes very little or becomes overly frustrated and cannot be patient enough to make the changes needed. The other scenario we often see is that the teacher goes immediately to the concerns that reside on the left end of the continuum. This is an understandable response. Surely this student needs to learn how to use spelling resources, how to put sentences together, and how to carefully consider word choice. However, no 5-minute conference is going to solve all these problems, and no doubt these concerns have probably already been noted to the student in many different contexts over his years as a struggling writer. It is the teacher's obligation to this student to give him high-level feedback that is concerned with those things on the right side of the continuum, and to work with him on conceptual ideas about writing as this teacher has. The teacher and instructional aide can continue the other work simultaneously, not necessarily on this paper at this point in the writing process, but in lots of instructional opportunities that arise during writing workshop or other writing instruction. Of course, this brief interaction won't solve the problems of his writing, either. But like his regularly achieving peers, this is the conversation that must begin his own growing understandings of the purpose and function of writing that is powerful and unique. The comments that the teacher selects, focused around Level 5, purpose, may be hard for the student to enact this time. This should not stop the teacher from providing this complex feedback.

7TH-GRADE WRITER

This last conference is with a 7th-grader who has strong writing skills. Her teacher has just finished reading her research paper arguing for the use of social media as a pedagogical tool. The student believes that students and teachers should be allowed to interact via Facebook and Twitter. Currently, doing so would be in violation of the school honor code. In this paper (omitted here for reasons of space), the teacher sees that the student has done appropriate research, has organized her argument and counterarguments logically, and uses an anecdote from her own life to draw the reader's interest. The teacher is accustomed to this student successfully communicating in writing and wants to be sure that she is given a challenge so that her revision is as robust as those of her less successful peers. This teacher also knows that conferences with strong students can be among the most challenging. It is very tempting to leave well enough alone and compliment the student on her skill. The teacher ends the conference with a concrete plan, however, for pushing the student into thinking through her writing on a very complicated level, one on which the student is clearly ready to engage.

> TEACHER: Like always, your work is really nice to read. You write in a clear and compelling way. Because you have so much skill in organizing and presenting ideas, I want to give you something to think about. You are writing about using social media in school, and you have given good reasons for doing that. If I went online and did a teeny bit of research, I bet I could find those same reasons, right? That is how you found them?

STUDENT: Well, no. First I thought them up and then I went to look for research to support my claim.

TEACHER: Even better. But since those ideas already exist in the world, I want you to think about the particular perspective you bring. Why should I listen to you, a teenager, when there are all these adults who have been to college telling me something else? I actually do think you have something important to say about it, but in addition to arguing for how you think things should be, you also are going to have to simultaneously argue for why we should listen to you. You are a good enough writer to do that. One way you might start is by doing some reading from current periodicals that make arguments. When you find one that really convinces you, see how the writer has established his or her credibility and place in the world relative to this topic.

Working with strong writers can be a significant challenge. It is always tempting to compliment them and move along. However, pushing student writers, no matter their level, is our obligation. This writer has shown what she can do; now it is time to test what she cannot. Without that challenge, she will not get the benefits of this very important instructional interaction.

CONCLUSION

The conferences between teachers and students above give a good idea of the kinds of feedback teachers can give in a stretch writing conference. The demands placed on these writers as they embark on their revisions are significant and in support of the expectations now placed on teaching and learning about writing.

Part III

IN SUPPORT OF GUIDED READING IN GRADES 3–8

Vast expectations are placed on teachers these days, and sometimes it feels as if the expectations shift daily, as standards, assessments, and curricula change. Though there may be a new "it" technique, methodology, or trend, we believe strongly that certain features of literacy instruction will always remain critical. Guided reading across the grades is one of those features. Students, regardless of age or ability, benefit from reading instruction that is tailored to their needs. Primary teachers see this most clearly, as some of their students come to them reading very well, even in kindergarten, while others come to them without even knowledge of the alphabet. Teachers know that they can't teach those two groups of students in the same way using the same materials, and so they differentiate their instruction accordingly. As students get older, though, and most of them begin to read more or less fluently, it becomes harder to see the differences. Often, teachers in grades 3–8 do not pull students into reading groups, assuming that they can support all students through whole-class instruction. Differentiation in the upper grades may only include a teacher sending her most struggling students to the reading resource room. The next three chapters provide a thorough overview that we hope will serve as a road map for making guided reading a regular and meaningful part of our readers' literacy instruction. Chapter 7 looks at the features of a balanced literacy classroom, and demonstrates how guided reading is nested within it. Chapter 8 looks at the procedures of guided reading and how to manage time during guided reading to prioritize time for one-on-one interactions. Chapter 9 focuses on the interactions themselves, providing multiple examples of stretch reading conferences, so that our readers will better understand the nature and depth of these interactions.

CHAPTER 7

Making a Space for Guided Reading in the Literacy Block

We understand how challenging it can be to consider making time and classroom space for work with small guided reading groups. In this chapter we will look at the intermediate and upper grade literacy block (or language arts classroom) and help teachers to understand where small-group or individualized differentiated reading instruction can fit into their literacy teaching.

BALANCED LITERACY INSTRUCTION

As important as guided reading is, we believe strongly that it is only effective when it is part of a balanced literacy classroom that also includes:

1. Shared reading
2. Independent reading
3. Independent literacy activities
4. Word study
5. Writing
6. Read-aloud

Each of these (except for writing, which was discussed in Chapters 4–6), will be described below, to clarify how guided reading can be nested into a teacher's overall literacy instruction. In Chapter 8, we will discuss how some teachers successfully build in weekly reading conferences with their students in lieu of (or sometimes in addition to) guided reading.

SHARED READING

Shared reading in grades 3 through
8 is generally a time when the
classroom teacher works with the
whole class to teach comprehension and vocabulary strategies.
One effective model that we have
observed includes such instructional moves as "think-aloud," or
cognitive modeling. In this teaching method, the teacher demonstrates strategies for her students
that allow them to perceive how
she makes sense of challenging texts. She then asks students what
they noticed about her reading and, finally, asks them to practice
one or more of the strategies they noticed during her demonstration. Figure 7.1, Architecture of a Shared Reading Think-Aloud
Lesson, displays one structure that we have found helpful in ac-
quainting teachers with the procedures of shared reading.

Explanation and example of a shared reading lesson. The steps of
the shared reading lesson, listed in Figure 7.1, are explained in detail below. In addition, an example of what a teacher would say is
given underneath each step. The teacher's words are in italics.

1. **Launch:** The teacher explains what she is about to do during the
   lesson. This helps prepare students for the kind of listening and
   noticing they will need to do.

   Okay, everyone . . . right now I'm going to become a reader. All
   my attention is going to be on reading and making sense out of
   this article. You'll notice that sometimes I look at the article
   and read the words on the page, and other times I look away and
   seem like I'm talking to myself. What I'm doing is revealing to
   you what's going on in my head when I read this article to help
   me better understand it. I want you to pay attention to what

Figure 7.1. Architecture of a Shared Reading Think-Aloud Lesson

1. *Launch*—here you explain what you are about to do, for example, "Now, I'm going to show you my thinking while I read. Watch what I'm doing to help myself understand this text, and when I'm done, I'm going to ask you to tell me what you noticed."
2. *Modeling*—now share what you're reading so that everyone can see it—this can be with a document camera or with multiple copies of a text. Make your thinking visible by talking about your thinking while you read. We believe it is best to utilize multiple strategies in order to give students a more realistic impression of what readers do when they're trying to make sense of a challenging text.
3. *Noticing*—students tell you what they noticed, and you write these down in order to create a list of strategies to be displayed in class.
4. *Guided Practice*—now ask students to try one of the strategies they saw you using. We recommend that guided practice be somewhat differentiated by using three different levels of text to best meet the needs of your above-, at-, and below-grade-level readers. During guided practice, you should walk around observing, prompting, and supporting student use of strategies.
5. *Extension*—remind students to remember these strategies when they are reading (during content-area reading, during independent reading, at home when they're doing their homework, and so on).

I'm saying while I read, because I'm going to ask you to tell me what you notice after I'm done reading. I've chosen an article about the 5-second rule, and I'm going to put it up on the board using the document camera so you can see it.

2. Modeling: Teacher shares what she is about to read so all the students can see it. This can be done with a document camera or with multiple copies of a text. The teacher makes thinking visible by talking about what she's thinking while she reads. It is best to utilize multiple strategies, in order to give students a more realistic impression of all the things readers do when they're trying to make sense of a challenging text.

First I'm going to look at the title of the article: "Study supports 5-second rule, but should you? Probably not." *Okay, well, I think the 5-second rule is that rule where you have 5 seconds to pick up a piece of food from the floor before it gets too germy, and this article appears to be reporting on a study that proves that the rule is true, but it's also telling me not to believe it. I'm going to keep reading.*

A new study appears to validate what every 12-year-old knows: If you drop food on the floor, you have 5 seconds until it becomes contaminated. *Okay, that's exactly what I got out of the title.*

Biology students at Aston University in Birmingham, England, tested the time-honored five-second rule and claim to have found some truth to it. The faster you pick food up off the floor, they discovered, the less likely it is to contain bacteria. *Okay, wait . . . I read that so fast that I think I missed the point, so I'm going to go back and read it again. All right, now I want to make sure I got it right, so I'm going to try to put that paragraph into my own words. In a nutshell, the 5-second rule has been tested by college students in England who have determined that the faster you pick food up off the floor, the less likely it is to have bacteria. But how did they figure it out, I wonder? Maybe if I keep reading, I'll find out.*

Working under the direction of microbiology professor Anthony Hilton, the students dropped toast, pasta, cookies and sticky candy and left them on the floor for three to 30 seconds . . . *Oh, okay, that sounds like an experiment for a class. Interesting. They dropped different items and left them on the floor for different amounts of time.*

. . . according to information released on the university's website March 10. *You know, this doesn't tell me much, just tells me where the information about the experiment was posted.*

They then monitored the transfer of two common bacteria, Escherichia coli and Staphylococcus aureus . . . *What? Those are crazy long scientific terms. I can't even say them, much less have any idea what they are. I'm going to keep reading to see if the author gives me more manageable information about those words.*

—in common terms, E. coli and staph. *Oh, that was nice of the author. She put the crazy long scientific terms in, but then she told me the more common words. E. coli and staph. I've heard of those, and I know that they are responsible for making a lot of people sick.*

The bacteria, they concluded, do a pretty lousy job at moving from floor to food, especially when the food isn't given much time to be a target. *This I understand. Even those nasty bacteria don't immediately jump onto my food, so it seems like if I pick my food up quickly, it might be safe to eat, even if there are terrible bacteria on my floor. Interesting.* (http://newsela.com/articles/fivesecond-rule/id/3179/)

3. **Noticing:** Students tell the teacher what they noticed during the think-aloud, and the teacher writes these down in order to create a list of comprehension strategies to be displayed in class.

Oh, boy . . . that was very interesting. I definitely would like to finish it another time. What did you notice me doing while I was reading it? I'm going to write what you noticed down on this chart paper so that you can refer back to it while you practice in a moment.

STUDENT 1: You reread once when you didn't remember what you read.

TEACHER: That's right, I read so fast and without thinking, that I completely missed what the paragraph said. What else?

STUDENT 2: You kept reading when you came to words you didn't know, to see if the author defined them.

TEACHER: Yes, she used the scientific terms, but then when I kept reading, I was happy to see that she also used the more common words, which I did understand. What else did you notice?

STUDENT 3: You read the title first and thought about it.

TEACHER: I did. It's always a good idea to look at the title, right? The title should give you a sneak preview of what's coming, and it's important to read it so you know what to expect. Anything else?

STUDENT 4: Sometimes you stopped and reviewed what you read before you went on reading.

TEACHER: Good, I did do that. When I'm reading about something I don't know much about, particularly science topics, I will stop at the end of a paragraph, or even sometimes at the end of a sentence, to put things into my own words to make sure I'm really understanding what I read.

4. **Guided Practice:** The teacher asks students to try one of the strategies they saw and heard her using during the think-aloud. Guided practice can be differentiated by using three different levels of text to best meet the needs of above-, at-, and below-grade-level readers. During guided practice, the teacher monitors and supports students as needed.

> *You did a great job noticing what I did while I was reading. Now, I'm going to give you all an article to read. I'm not giving you all the same article, because I tried to find articles that would provide a challenge for each of you. I want you to start reading these articles, and I'd like you to use the strategies that you noticed me using today. In particular, I'd like you to try to stop reading after each paragraph to think through what you just read before you continue. Pay attention to the strategies you use to make sense of reading, because I'm going to walk around and ask what you're doing to make sense of your article.*

5. **Extension:** Upon completion of guided practice, the teacher concludes the lesson by reminding the students that these strategies can be used throughout their reading day.

> *Well done, everyone. I really liked seeing how you used some of the strategies you noticed me using while you read your articles. Remember to use these strategies later, in science and even social studies, because they will help you to make sense of our textbooks.*

This is but one of many models for shared reading. Whatever model a teacher elects, the purpose of shared reading is to offer students greater understanding and experience in the use of strategies to discern the meaning of difficult texts.

GUIDED READING

During shared reading, teachers model and have students practice using specific comprehension strategies. It is done with the whole group because the strategies that students need to utilize to make sense of text are the same no matter what their reading level is. In guided reading, however, teachers must work with small homogeneous groups in order to more closely monitor how students utilize strategies when they read. Chapter 8 will provide a very detailed look at the structure and procedures of guided reading.

> **COMMON CORE CONNECTION**
>
> Guided reading is the ideal time to introduce students to complex texts that they may not be able to read independently. During guided reading, teachers can provide the scaffolding that is needed to help even their struggling readers handle the demands of complex texts.

Here, we simply want to make sure our readers understand how guided reading fits into the literacy block.

Guided reading in the upper elementary and intermediate grades is a time to meet with students to support their comprehension of challenging texts. The goal during guided reading is to see how well students can tap into the arsenal of comprehension strategies teachers have taught during shared reading. Students need not utilize the specific strategy that was taught during shared reading that day, although teachers may prompt them to do so if it would help. Rather, teachers try to make sure that students are utilizing any strategy that will help them in a specific moment. During guided reading, teachers provide a text they believe will challenge students with regard to content and structure. Because comprehension should be the focus, teachers should choose texts that are challenging to understand.

When teachers listen to individual students read aloud and then ask questions about the text, they notice what students are able to do to make sense of the text, and what challenges them. Teachers can suggest strategies that will help students overcome those challenges in the moment and into the future. During guided reading, teachers also take anecdotal notes about their students' reading in order to be able to consider, over time, how students are developing in their use of specific strategies. As guided reading conferences are the focus of the next chapters, we will leave the details for the present time. Please see Chapter 8 in particular for much more discussion of the role of guided reading and processes of guided reading for fluent readers.

INDEPENDENT READING

The ultimate goal for children is that they become lifelong readers who read for a variety of reasons both in and out of school. For that reason, teachers must provide time for students to read independently during school. With a well-stocked library containing books and magazines on a wide range of topics that represent diverse ideas and backgrounds, as well as a wide range of levels appropriate to the readers in the class, students can find or be guided by the teacher to materials that will engage them and pull them into the world of reading.

Independent reading is also a time when teachers can explicitly remind their students to use strategies they have learned during shared reading and practiced during guided reading to make sense of books on their own, with no support from the teacher. Students don't always connect what they learn during whole-group instruction to their own independent reading, and helping students understand the progression of learning from teacher-directed, to guided, to independent will increase their understanding of ways in which they can employ strategies when reading on their own.

Finally, independent reading can be a critical component within a classroom because it is a time when students can productively engage in a literacy activity without teacher intervention. In order to allow the teacher time to work with small groups, the whole group must be self-managing. There are many ways that teachers can occupy the rest of their class when they work with small groups, but few are as simple, yet beneficial, as independent reading. We often tell teachers that if they can get their students to read independently for at least 20 minutes at a time, then they can pull a group for guided reading.

We believe strongly that all language arts classrooms must provide shared reading, guided reading, and independent reading, because they are interconnected, as shown in Figure 7.2. Though modeling comprehension and vocabulary strategies during shared reading is critical to helping students understand what readers can do to make sense of a challenging text, without opportunities to practice that strategy with and without teacher support, it is meaningless. Similarly, doing guided reading with students who haven't seen an expert (e.g., the teacher) utilize reading strategies isn't nearly as meaningful as it is when students develop a common un-

Figure 7.2. Interdependence of Shared, Guided, and Independent Reading

Shared Reading	Guided Reading	Independent Reading
→		
Teacher modeling of comprehension and vocabulary strategies. A time to introduce or reintroduce strategies.	Students read challenging texts in order to utilize necessary reading strategies with teacher support.	Students read on their own for pleasure and to apply strategies they have learned and used during shared and guided reading.

derstanding and language about reading strategies through shared reading. Finally, students must be given opportunities to take what is learned during shared reading and reinforced during guided reading to practice on their own during independent reading. Getting students to be successful and engaged while they read on their own is why we teach reading.

INDEPENDENT LITERACY ACTIVITIES

Teachers cannot pull small groups for guided reading (just as they cannot pull students for writing conferences) unless they have procedures in place for independent literacy work. As we mentioned above, independent reading can serve several pedagogical purposes, including providing students with something to do when teachers are working with small groups. We always recommend that teachers who have had difficulty enacting independent literacy work (e.g., centers, stations, or Daily 5 in Boushey & Moser, 2014) start by simply building students' stamina for reading independently. Once students can read for 20-minute stretches consistently, teachers can begin doing guided reading. Beyond that, teachers can also work to build students' capacity to write independently (as described in Chapter 4). Once students can consistently write independently for 20-minute stretches, teachers can begin pulling additional guided reading groups. Though we believe that working with two guided reading groups per day is sufficient, teachers can add variation to

Figure 7.3. Daily Guided Reading Block

First 20-Minute Block of Time	Short Break	Second 20-Minute Block of Time
Teacher works with first guided reading group. Rest of the class reads independently.	5 minutes or less during which teacher may read aloud, students stand up and stretch, etc.	Teacher works with second guided reading group. Rest of the class writes independently.

independent literacy activities, as advocated by Boushey and Moser (2014). Variations might include word work, listening to reading, and partner reading. The most important thing is that any independent time be worthwhile and supportive of students' development as readers and writers.

One model for guided reading combined with independent literacy work that we believe is manageable for most teachers is shown in Figure 7.3.

OTHER IMPORTANT ASPECTS OF THE LITERACY BLOCK

Chapters 4 and 5 focused upon writing instruction, another integral part of literacy instruction. Word study in the intermediate and upper elementary grades remains important, though for most students, the emphasis changes from phonology to vocabulary study. Struggling readers often need support with decoding, and teachers can address those issues through routine and regular time devoted to word sorts and other word study activities. *Words Their Way* (Bear, Invernizzi, Templeton, & Johnston, 2011) does a fine job helping teachers sort out how best to address the spelling and vocabulary needs of upper elementary and intermediate grade students.

Finally, teachers of grades 3–8 should remember just how important it is for students to have opportunities to listen to excellent and engaging literature and nonfiction books through teacher read-alouds. Although primary teachers engage in this practice throughout their school day, in the upper grades it sometimes drops off. Researchers (Albright & Ariail, 2005; Ivey & Broaddus, 2001) suggest that reading aloud is beneficial to students of all ages.

It provides an opportunity for students to simply enjoy and engage with great books. It exposes them to important vocabulary and concepts, and it provides a model for fluent reading. Further, it exposes students to books that they might not be able to read on their own, a critical need for struggling readers.

CHAPTER 8

Structuring Reading Conferences During Guided Reading

Once teachers have made space and time for guided reading in their classrooms, they begin considering how to use that time as efficiently and meaningfully as possible. In Chapter 3, we discussed using the Continuum of Task Complexity During Guided Reading to prompt high-quality interactions about reading. In this chapter, we lay out procedures for guided reading that highlight its essential features and prioritize the individual student-teacher interactions.

GUIDED READING: ESSENTIAL BUT BRIEF

We believe that guided reading (or differentiated small-group work), a time for teachers to support students as they try out a variety of strategies for making meaning of texts, is an essential part of the literacy block in grades 3–8. We know that middle school teachers in particular, who usually have a shorter time period to work with students each day, often wonder how to fit guided reading into their language arts instruction. It is with this concern in mind that we created a structure for guided reading that includes its most critical aspects while whittling down the time needed to do it. We think 20 minutes for a group of five students is about right, and doable. Most teachers find working with two groups per day manageable, while middle school teachers with only 45–60 minutes may meet only one group per day and see only three groups per week. As mentioned in Chapter 7, guided reading is only feasible once students are able to engage in independent literacy activities (such as independent reading and writing) for 20 minutes at a time, so that the teacher can concentrate on the reading challenges presented by students in the guided reading group.

Structure of Guided Reading. Understandings of what guided reading should entail differ wildly. Indeed, even within a single school, guided reading can be enacted in very different ways. While we acknowledge the strengths of many different models for guided reading and have learned much from them, our structure for guided reading places most of the emphasis on the interactions teachers have with students, while minimizing or eliminating any pre-reading activities. We interpret the term *guided reading* literally: This is the time for teachers to guide students' reading. We do not believe that this is the time to teach a lesson on reading strategies or vocabulary, as that can be done during shared reading.

The following provides a brief outline and explanation of our structure for guided reading (refer to Berne & Degener, 2010, 2012 for much more information about this structure). It is important to note that it can be challenging to stick to the precise timing at first. Teachers new to this structure often bring a timer or stopwatch to the guided reading group to help keep themselves on track. Over time and with practice, teachers find the timing much more manageable.

1. Teacher introduces reading material and reminds students of a useful strategy for reading it (1 minute).
2. Teacher reads a sentence or two aloud, and may also ask the group to chorally read a sentence or two aloud, as a warmup (1 minute).
3. Teacher directs students to read at their own pace, reminding them to make sure to attend to meaning as they read (less than 1 minute).
4. Teacher conferences with each individual student, one at a time, while the other students read to themselves (3 minutes per student, about 15 minutes total).
5. Students stop reading and report back to the other group members what they worked on during their conference with the teacher and what strategy they used (about 3 minutes).

The reporting serves as an important reinforcement of the work they did, and also offers the other students a review of appropriate meaning-making strategies.

Notice that most of the teacher's time is spent conferencing with students. During guided reading conferences, teachers can assess how students are making meaning of what they read by asking probing questions to check understanding and prompting students to utilize appropriate meaning-making strategies.

Teacher-Student Interactions. In grades 3–8, the instructional emphasis during guided reading is always comprehension. This is true regardless of student ability. Struggling readers deserve dedicated time devoted to improving their comprehension skills just like their peers who read at and above grade level. Teachers of struggling readers will want to consider how they can carve out time to address word-level concerns (such as decoding, vocabulary, and fluency) during other parts of the literacy block so that guided reading can be entirely devoted to comprehension. For the very rare complete nonreader, comprehension is best scaffolded through listening. In a guided reading setting, the teacher can read the text to the student, ask questions, and prompt to support listening comprehension.

Students who have grown accustomed to heavy teacher support around decoding or vocabulary concerns during guided reading may initially have a hard time when comprehension becomes the primary focus. They are not used to paying attention to meaning, and therefore may be unsure how to respond to deeper comprehension questions. Initially, teachers should expect to provide much scaffolding to support such students' meaning-making capabilities.

Materials for Guided Reading. In order for students to be ready for the demands of content-area learning, as emphasized in the Common Core State Standards, more attention than ever is being placed on the reading of informational texts. Guided reading is an ideal time for supporting this shift.

Teachers often have a lot of questions about locating appropriate materials for students during guided reading. A good rule of thumb is that teachers should choose reading material that provides a challenge to students. This should be a comprehension challenge, meaning that students should be able to read most of the individual words relatively easily so that they can concentrate on making meaning. Providing struggling readers with texts that they can capably decode does not dumb down their instruction, but actually allows them the opportunity to make complicated meaning rather than just practice decoding. For readers of average achievement, materials that are more challenging than they can read on their own are generally appropriate. Teachers of very skilled readers may need to look beyond classroom sets of leveled texts to newspaper or magazine articles that will provide a significant and authentic challenge. Here is a list of materials that teachers may find useful:

newsela.com: This is an online source of articles, culled from newspapers across the country, on a wide variety of topics. What makes it notable is that the website's staff rewrites the articles at a variety of levels.

Scholastic's Scope: Middle school teachers rave about this magazine from Scholastic. It comes in print as well as online. Its articles, written in graphically appealing ways about topics of interest to adolescents, are perfect for use during guided reading.

Storyworks: Another Scholastic magazine, this one is appropriate for grades 3–6, and contains fiction and nonfiction pieces that appeal to students.

Time for Kids: This newsmagazine comes in print and online form, and provides a look at national news and topics of interest to students in grades 3–6.

Online newspapers: For older students and more proficient readers, we recommend using online articles and op-ed pieces from local newspapers as well as the *New York Times, USA Today,* the *Wall Street Journal,* and so forth. These provide a never-ending source of reading material on topics of local and national interest.

In addition to these resources, there are many online sites devoted to science and current events, as well as blogs on topics of interest to students, including nutrition, sports, education, music, and so on.

WHAT TAKES PLACE DURING GUIDED READING?

Beginning the Guided Reading Group

The teacher starts guided reading by introducing students to the text they will be reading, and offering a suggestion for a strategy that may be of use while they read. She might say something like, "Today we will be reading an article about the Mars Rover. This article has a lot of scientific terminology. Although you may not be able to understand each word, stop reading after each paragraph and see if you can put the information into your own words so that you can make sure you're making sense as you read." This strategy reminder likely mirrors a strategy she has modeled during shared reading, and she is reminding them to apply what they have been practicing. She does not teach new strategies during this time.

Next, the teacher may read a bit of the article aloud, to orient everyone to the reading. She may also ask students to read a small amount chorally, again to orient them to the reading. Before the students begin reading on their own, the teacher reminds them of their task for the remainder of the time. "Now I want you to read the rest on your own, at your own pace. Remember that I chose this article because I thought it would be a challenge for you. Remember to employ any of the reading strategies we have worked on in order to make meaning of this text."

One-on-One Interactions During Guided Reading

As described in the procedures for guided reading detailed above, the teacher meets with each student in the group individually in a guided reading conference. These interactions proceed in the same fashion each time. First, the teacher asks the student to begin reading. Many teachers ask students to read from wherever they happen to be, while others specify a place to begin reading. This reading should be brief because the entire conference will last only about 3 minutes. Because the focus is the kind of deep comprehension that stretches a student's thinking, the teacher need not wait until the student stumbles or miscues. In fact, we have found it best to stop the student's reading rather quickly. However, there are some clues from student reading that may indicate a comprehension breakdown. In other work, we have referred to this as the four "P's" (see Berne & Degener, 2012):

- *Pace:* When students read much more quickly or more slowly than they usually do, it can be a sign that they are not attending to meaning as they read.
- *Punctuation:* When students ignore punctuation, reading through periods and commas, that is also a sign that they are not making meaning. Conversely, students who stop at the end of each line, whether there's a period or not, are probably not attending to meaning.
- *Prosody:* Another thing to listen for is the degree to which students read in a monotone or stilted voice, ignoring the phrasing of the passage (though for some students, this is the way they read aloud no matter what).
- *Pushing past errors:* If students read a word incorrectly and do not notice and/or make no effort to fix the word, it could be because they are not making meaning.

Any of the issues above can indicate a lack of comprehension, and it is particularly important to stop a student's reading before they have read too much if their reading displays one or more of the four "P's." On the other hand, students can read fluently, and with perfect phrasing, and still not have any idea what they have just read, so a good rule of thumb is to stop a student's reading after no more than a paragraph.

After listening to the student read, the teacher asks a question to determine how well he understood the passage. The teacher may use what she notices about the student's reading in considering what to say to him. For example, if she notices that the student is reading much faster than usual, she might say: "Wow, you read that so fast! I could barely follow you, and I am wondering if you were able to follow this. Can talk me through what you just read?" Or, "I noticed that you had trouble with a couple of words. I'm wondering if you can tell me the most important ideas in this passage, even though you didn't recognize all the words."

If the student reads fluently and the teacher doesn't notice any problem, she still asks the same kind of questions. For example, "You read that paragraph quite well, but there is a lot of information here. Could you please talk me through the most important ideas you just read?"

Generally speaking, there are four possible outcomes after the teacher asks the student a question:

1. The student is not able to answer the question at all.
2. The student gives an incorrect answer.
3. The student is able to give a partial answer.
4. The student answers the question to the teacher's satisfaction.

Consider these four outcomes and how the teacher would respond in each situation.

Scenario 1: The student can't answer the question at all. In this situation, the teacher needs to consider what would help the student most. Usually, when a student can't even begin to answer the question, it means the student wasn't truly attending while reading. The best strategy here is to prompt the student to reread, as in the following example:

The student has just read the following passage on tegu lizards (https://newsela.com/articles/environment-tegulizard/id/1336/). His reading was a bit halting in parts, but he had no trouble decoding.

The tegus found in the wild most likely were abandoned by their owners. Although wild reptiles, the lizards have become popular pets. They also may have escaped from breeding centers in south Miami-Dade County.

Wildlife experts are trying to round up as many tegus as possible before October, when the lizards go into hibernation. After that, it will be difficult to find them.

And they're especially worried that the black-and-white tegus will spread to nearby Everglades National Park. A handful of them already have been caught there. The lizards eat just about anything. Their menu includes small animals, birds, insects, plants, and their all-time favorite—eggs. And that means goodbye to the baby American crocodiles that hatch in the refuge and other endangered animals like the wood rat.

TEACHER: I'm impressed with how you tackled this passage! I know there were some new ideas in there. I'm wondering if you can talk me through what you just read about tegu lizards so that I can better understand this.

STUDENT (long pause): I don't really remember what I just read.

TEACHER: That's okay. I appreciate your honesty. Lots of times, I read a paragraph and then get to the end and think, "I have no idea what I just read!" That happens. Do you have any idea what you could do now so that you might remember and understand the passage better?

STUDENT: I could go back and reread it.

TEACHER: That's right! Why don't you do that right now? This time, as you're reading, remember that you're trying to make sense of this passage. Probably you're going to have to read it more slowly.

Note that in this situation, the teacher does two things. First of all, she asks the student if he can think of something to do rather than telling him what to do. The goal of the guided reading stretch conference is to support students as they make meaning. Often that means allowing them to think through a solution even if it might be more expedient to directly instruct. However, had the student not been able to come up with a strategy, the teacher could have prompted him.

Second, the teacher asks the student to demand more from his own reading. The student read the passage fluently, but didn't make meaning. In guiding the student to reread, the teacher reminds him that the ultimate goal of reading is comprehension.

Scenario 2: The student gives an incorrect answer. Often when teachers ask a question during guided reading, they note that a student has missed some very important information in the passage. One of the best ways to address this is to ask the student where in the text he found his information. Consider the following scenario, in which the student is responding to the same teacher question as above, "Could you talk me through what you just read about tegu lizards?"

> STUDENT: Well, these tegu lizards are wild lizards that are eating a lot of animals, including pets and some other animals in the wild.
>
> TEACHER: Really? Where in the text does it say that tegu lizards are wild animals that are eating pets? Will you go back and find that part?
>
> STUDENT (rereading to himself): Oh! It doesn't exactly say that. It says that they used to be wild but they're becoming popular pets. They're not eating pets!
>
> TEACHER: Okay, good. You see how important it is to really self-monitor while you're reading? You read the words well, but you weren't really paying attention to how the words were connecting. Sometimes I check in with myself after every couple of sentences, just to make sure I'm understanding what I read. I'd like you to do that as you continue reading, okay? After every sentence or two, stop and make sure you really understood.

Like the previous student, this student now also understands that the goal of reading is accurate meaning-making.

Scenario 3: The student gives a partial answer. Often students read a passage and retain some information about it that they can tell the teacher afterward. Consider this scenario, referring to the same passage about tegu lizards:

> The student reads and has few decoding issues.
>
> TEACHER: You read that well. I wonder if you can share with me what you learned in this passage.
>
> STUDENT: Well, it's about these animals called tegu lizards.
>
> TEACHER: That's right, but what can you tell me about these lizards?
>
> STUDENT: Well, they used to be pets, but now they're in the wild.

Often teachers are perfectly satisfied with this kind of answer. The student read the passage fluently and showed at least some comprehension of the passage. However, teachers should ensure that students are able to demonstrate a deeper understanding by asking follow-up stretch questions such as the following:

TEACHER: That's true. Why does this matter? What's the big deal?
STUDENT: I'm not really sure. They're trying to catch them?
TEACHER: Yes. Why do you think they're trying to catch them? The person who wrote this article thinks that this is an important topic, and I want to see if you can find out why. Read through this passage again, and tell me before you do what information you will be trying to discover.
STUDENT: Why they're trying to catch the lizards?
TEACHER: Exactly.

This is an effective interaction because the teacher stretches the student's understanding beyond the surface level. Students will sometimes look down at the passage they've just read and pull out just enough information to satisfy the teacher. This is a strategy that students often use because they want to provide a correct answer, even when they haven't constructed a deep understanding of the text. It takes a bit more time to determine if students have really understood, but it is time well spent. In this scenario, the teacher prompts the student to set a purpose for reading, which should help him seek out a more complex understanding.

Scenario 4: The student answers questions satisfactorily. Teachers often ask us what to do when students are able to answer all the questions that they have asked fully and correctly. Indeed, this can be a frustrating scenario for teachers, who know that their job during guided reading is to stretch students' thinking with texts and tasks that are more complex than those that they would be able to complete on their own. Here, though, we provide some suggestions for what to say to students who have demonstrated relatively thorough comprehension. Keeping the passage on tegu lizards in mind, consider the following scenario:

The student reads the passage fluently.

TEACHER: Will you talk me through what you just read?

STUDENT: Sure. Well, there are these lizards called tegu lizards in Florida. And I guess they used to be wild, but then they were kept as pets. Anyway, apparently a lot of them have escaped and they're now eating other small animals in the Everglades, including eggs, and that's bad, because some of the animals are endangered. They're trying to catch them before they start hibernating, because then they'll be really hard to find.

TEACHER: Wow, you really provided me a good overview of everything you read.

When teachers are faced with this kind of comprehension, they often don't know what their next move should be. Some teachers will ask the student to keep reading, to see if there may be something more challenging for the student to comprehend in the next paragraph. Though this impulse is understandable, the result can be that the interaction with this particular student will extend too long without the student ever facing a challenge. Instead, the teacher might say one of two things. First of all, it is perfectly reasonable to respond the way the teacher above did, and just compliment the student on her reading. The teacher can take the compliment even further by asking the student something like, "Wow, you read that well. What did you do while you were reading or what strategy did you use to make sense of this as you read?" Such a question still asks the student to be mindful of the strategies she used while reading, and helps the teacher to check the student's awareness of her own reading process.

Using another approach, the teacher can ask a stretch question that goes beyond the text at hand, to see if the student is able to consider the significance of the text in the greater world. For example, the teacher could say, "How is this passage like what we read in science about nonnative plants in the prairie?" This question encourages the student to consider connections between a content-area topic he has previously studied and the text at hand. Note that students may not be able to answer these kinds of questions the first time they are asked. However, these kinds of questions help students better understand the complexity of reading, and over time, students begin to deepen their understanding of what it means to be a reader.

It is certainly not our goal to trick a child or make him think he doesn't understand something that he, in fact, does. However, texts can be read on many levels, and advanced readers have the opportunity to be pushed toward even greater meaning-making challenges. Finally, a teacher who works with a child who repeatedly understands texts quite completely should also consider finding more challenging texts. This is why we encourage text-sharing across grades.

Keep in mind that Chapter 9 will delve more deeply into conferences during guided reading, and will provide more examples of how teachers can stretch students' understanding in meaningful ways.

Concluding the Guided Reading Group

Because the purpose of guided reading is to support students' deep understanding of texts and practice using strategies, the final 3 minutes of guided reading are spent reviewing interactions. This allows students time to share their struggles with one another and how they remedied them. In doing so, they share their reading strategies with one another, which serves to reinforce the strategy and to introduce the other students to a strategy of which they may not be aware. Students really enjoy this sharing time. Far from making them self-conscious about the errors they made, students seem to take pride in the work they did to fix their problems. Most students, too, enjoy their short time in the spotlight, when everyone is paying attention to them. One thing that surprises teachers is that students, regardless of age, almost always remember what they worked on with the teacher, as well as the strategy they utilized to work out a problem area. We do recommend that teachers take brief anecdotal notes during this time (described in the section below) so that they can remind students of what they worked on, in case they forget, and so that they themselves can remember in the days and weeks ahead. The notes serve as prompts, also, for follow-up whole-group instruction.

The final interaction looks something like the following:

TEACHER: Great job reading today, everybody. Now we're going to take the last few minutes to think about what you worked on with me today, and any strategies you used to make sense of this text. Brandon, do you remember what you worked on?

BRANDON: I read this part here about tegu lizards in the Everglades. I wasn't sure why people were trying to catch them, so I went back and reread, thinking about that question in particular.

TEACHER: That's right . . . so you did do that?

BRANDON: Yes, and I was able to find out why.

TEACHER: Great! It's always a good idea to read with a purpose in mind, and when you're not sure about what happened in the text, it's important to go back and reread. What about you, Tamika? (And the interactions continue with each student in the group, until everyone has shared.)

Often students have worked on the same kinds of strategies, and the teacher can help them to see this. The teacher then sends the students back to their seats with the reminder that the strategies they used in the group are strategies they can use when they are reading at home or in another class.

FORMATIVE ASSESSMENT DURING GUIDED READING

When guided reading is conducted as described above, it can serve not only as instructional support for the student, but also as a means of formative assessment, individually and across students. Each and every time a teacher listens to a student read and asks questions about that reading, she learns valuable information about that student as a reader that serves, over time, to paint a more complete portrait both of him and of his reading abilities. Immediately following each individual conference, the teacher should take some time to jot down notes before working with the next student. Each teacher has notions about how best to organize this information. Some teachers take notes on large note cards, with one card for each student, which they keep on a ring. Other teachers keep notes in a binder, with one page devoted to each student's reading. Others still take notes on Post-its and then store those Post-its in a binder or other notebook. However teachers choose to organize the information, it is helpful to include the following:

- Name of student
- Date

- Title of text or article read
- Level, if available
- Noted strengths
- Challenge faced during reading, along with prompt supplied to help student with that challenge

By keeping these kinds of notes, teachers can track their students' progress, noting how the strengths change over time, what strategies seem to help students most, and which strategies seem hard to implement successfully. The teacher can also look across students to see what struggles they have in common, and then provide appropriate whole-class instruction.

Some teachers also ask students to take similar kinds of notes in their own guided reading notebooks so that students, too, can be aware of their successes and struggles over time.

ONE-ON-ONE CONFERENCES IN LIEU OF GUIDED READING

We have been approached by middle school teachers who have asked us why they need to do guided reading groups when they believe that they could accomplish these one-on-one conferences outside of the group. This *is* possible, but taking students out of the group and traveling to each student individually can be less efficient. Time is at a premium in the intermediate and upper grades, and it is easier to manage meeting with five groups of five each week than to make time for 25 individual conferences. The conclusion of guided reading groups, when students get to share what they worked on and take ownership of their own meaning-making, is also highly valuable. That being said, it is true that teachers can accomplish most of the same goals in one-on-one conferences.

Traditionally, individual reading conferences have been a time for students and teachers to have a pleasant conversation about a high-interest book of the student's own choosing. We value those conferences and don't want guided reading conferences to replace them. Teachers who can find a way to do both should be careful to distinguish the purpose of each for the students.

CHAPTER 9

Students and Teachers Conference About Reading

Chapter 7 provided a look at where guided reading fits into literacy instruction in grades 3–8, and Chapter 8 provided an explanation of how teachers can structure guided reading to be time-efficient as well as focused primarily on meaning-centered individual interactions with students, which we have called stretch conferences. We hope that these two chapters have convinced our readers of the importance of continuing to work with students in small, homogeneous groups, in order to reinforce and support students' use of comprehension strategies in individualized ways.

This chapter focuses largely on examples of stretch conferences during guided reading, in order to clarify exactly what these entail. It is our experience that teachers can readily be convinced that guided reading is an important part of their literacy instruction, and they can learn the procedures to make it efficient and highly focused on individual student needs. However, once they get the structures of guided reading in place and develop confidence in their ability to group kids and choose materials, they struggle with what to say to students. As Chapter 3 noted, teachers find it relatively easy to support students' decoding errors or vocabulary struggles. Similarly, they can easily ask a factual comprehension question on the spot and can just as easily ascertain if the student can answer it. It is much harder to ask questions about and ascertain students' understanding of more complex textual ideas. In trying to help teachers with this, we developed the Continuum of Task Complexity During Guided Reading, which was explained in Chapter 3. Figure 9.1 reviews the interactions described in that chapter.

To reiterate points made in previous chapters, it can be immediately satisfying and rewarding to work in the first three levels of

Figure 9.1. Review of the Continuum of Task Complexity During Guided Reading

Level 1 *Word-Level Decoding*	I heard you pronounce this word as *organs*. I understand why, because look (teacher covers up the end of the word): This word begins with the letters from *organ*. Let's cover up *organ* and look at the rest of the word. What do you see?
Level 2 *Word-Level Vocabulary*	What vocabulary strategy that we have learned about might help you figure out the meaning of that word?
Level 3 *Sentence-Level Comprehension*	You read that very well. Do you remember how many bacteria there are on Earth?
Level 4 *Cumulative Comprehension*	You just read a lot of information about bacteria. Help me to understand this passage by talking me through the main ideas you just read about.
Level 5 *Critical Understanding*	What do you think would happen if bacteria were somehow removed from a person's body?
Level 6 *Discerning Greater Meaning*	I want you to consider how this article intersects with the recent phenomenon of making hand soaps and other cleaning products antibacterial.

the continuum. Teachers can easily ascertain when a problem has occurred for a student by either noticing when that student mispronounces or stumbles over a word, pronounces a challenging word correctly but hesitantly, or reads so quickly or slowly that comprehension probably hasn't taken place. Being able to help a child pronounce a word they didn't know, make sense of a challenging vocabulary word, or reread in order to answer a factual comprehension question can be a fulfilling experience. The teacher knows immediately that she has helped the student with something he didn't know or couldn't do before. Nevertheless, we encourage teachers to ask more of their students, concentrating their guided reading conferences on Levels 4, 5, and 6.

As noted in Chapters 3 and 8, teachers must be mindful of the expectations they have had for students in the past as they consider what they might demand of those students during stretch conferences. For example, if a struggling reader has been asked to tackle word-level demands almost exclusively during guided reading, it would be an unreasonable leap to begin asking that student to "discern greater meaning" from texts. Teachers may need to build up to Level 5 and Level 6 questions for some students. It is important to make sure that students can first demonstrate cumulative understanding. In addition, teachers must remember that students may not be able to demonstrate an immediate ability to do what is asked of them. Part of the premise of the stretch conference is that it will be a cognitive stretch for the student, and it may be, particularly at first, that the student will leave the interaction uncertain about what he learned as a reader in that moment. Over time, as students realize that they are being asked to think more deeply about texts than previously, they will be able to tackle the demands more successfully.

STRETCH CONFERENCES DURING GUIDED READING

One of the teachers with whom we worked confessed to us that she often had trouble knowing what to say to students during guided reading to support their comprehension of text beyond factual understanding. She made an observation that we believe to be extremely important: "I think my issue during guided reading is, I honestly don't know enough about what *I do* to comprehend text to be able to help students do it." We appreciated that insight because it helped us think about the kind of support we could provide for teachers to help them better understand the processes of comprehension. One of the things we encourage teachers to do is use materials during shared reading that provide a genuine challenge, not only for their students but for them as well. Doing a think-aloud with text that challenges them requires teachers to really tap into the strategies they utilize in making sense of text. This will serve them well during guided reading, because they can share with the students the parallels between the challenges the students currently face and the challenges they themselves faced during shared reading. Knowing that all readers struggle sometimes (even their teacher) can be very liberating for students.

In addition, we recommend that teachers carefully read the texts they are going to use during guided reading so that they have a good understanding of (1) the content of the text and how different parts of the text connect to one another, and (2) what factors contribute to the complexity of the text. There are many things that can make a text complex, including unfamiliar content, lack of prior knowledge, vocabulary, syntax, genre, and structure.

When teachers examine a text and determine why it may be complex for one of their students, they can both stretch their student's thinking and provide the support that will help the student overcome that complexity. For example, consider the following passage read by an advanced 8th-grade student (retrieved from www. scribd.com/doc/97103530/ Elephant-Dissertation):

> The sound structure of elephants is very much advanced. Over the course of the past few decades, there have been many studies completed on the infrasound hearing capabilities of elephants. [. . .]
>
> Interestingly, in the book *Elephants* by Eltringham, a passage on an elephant's hearing is described in full in the following passage: "The elephant is usually considered to have an acute sense of hearing, although firm data on the matter are hard to find. The large pinnae are not necessarily indicative of good hearing because their primary functions lie in temperature control and social signaling. Elephants do not appear to communicate over long distances, so perhaps there is little need for particularly good hearing, but it is difficult to be certain whether an elephant has not heard a distant sound or is simply ignoring it."
>
> Luckily it was discovered that this was totally wrong and that elephants do communicate over huge distances.

Looking at that text ahead of time, a teacher would notice that there is some science-specific vocabulary such as *pinnae* that might be confusing to students. In addition, the sentence structure is complicated, with many ideas combined into single sentences. Finally, there is a great deal of text devoted to discussion of an idea that appears to have been disproven. The overall structure of the text is therefore complex and somewhat deceptive, as one reads and tries to make sense of the information in the second paragraph, only to find out in the third paragraph that it is incorrect information.

Suppose a teacher listens to one of her students read the passage, and asks a question that taps into Level 4, cumulative comprehension.

> TEACHER: You read that well, Deanna. I know there were probably some words in there that you didn't recognize, because they are very specific to the study of elephants. I'm not going to worry so much about those now, but I'd like you to talk me through what you just read so that I can make sure you understood the big ideas about elephants and their hearing.
>
> STUDENT: Well, like you said, this is all about how elephants hear, and it seems like the scientists are interested in knowing more about that. I think this says that elephants hear pretty well, but their large pinnae—and I think that means their big ears but I'm not sure—do not actually lead to better hearing. Also, elephants don't communicate with each other from far away.

Since the teacher understands, having read this passage previously, that the second paragraph is dense and full of complex sentences that require much cognitive energy on the part of the student reading it, she also knows that it is entirely possible that the student may completely miss the final paragraph that lets the reader know that the second paragraph contained false information. So, she may say something like the following:

> TEACHER: You did a good job making sense of what was said in this long paragraph. And yes, I do think pinnae refer to the elephant's ears. I'm going to tell you that the author did something a bit sneaky in writing this piece. Did you pay attention to what he wrote in the last paragraph? [The student looks at the last paragraph again.]
>
> STUDENT: Oh, man . . . it seems like the author is saying that everything I read in this paragraph has been proven false.
>
> TEACHER: That is right. I'm not really sure why the author did that, but now I am going to ask you again to talk me through this passage and tell me what you know about elephant hearing.

STUDENT: Well, I don't know much! I guess I know now that elephants do communicate across long distances, but I don't know if it's due to their big ears or not.

TEACHER: You're right. From the part that you've read so far, you don't know as much about elephant hearing as you thought you did. You've got to be careful when you're reading complicated texts. Even though the author won't always trick you like this, you need to be mindful of how each paragraph connects with the other paragraphs. It's not enough to understand one paragraph. You need to think about how they all fit together to inform you about a topic.

Consider how this stretch conference scripted above compares with the following interaction that might predictably occur in some classes:

TEACHER: You did good reading of this passage. It's pretty complicated. I noticed that you stumbled a bit over this word, even though you said it correctly. *Pinnae.* Have you heard that word before?

STUDENT: No, I haven't.

TEACHER: What do you think it refers to?

STUDENT: Well, I think it may be referring to the elephant's ears, because they talk about the size and they're also talking about hearing in this paragraph.

TEACHER: That's great. You were able to infer from the paragraph and the overall context that pinnae refer to the elephant's ears.

Though the teacher in the second interaction may feel satisfied that she has accomplished something that helped the student's reading, the interaction does not leave the student with a better understanding of how she might navigate a text like this one. It hasn't stretched the student's thinking about the complexity of reading.

For the remainder of this chapter, we will provide some examples from our own observations of teachers working with students. (Please note that in most cases, these interactions are re-created based on our observation notes, and are not direct transcriptions.) We suggest to our readers that they read through the text excerpts first and consider what makes them complex, prior to reading the teacher-student interaction about the text.

5TH-GRADE GUIDED READING GROUP

Text used: A portion of an article titled "Women Flying High," from *Time for Kids*, June 17, 2013

Looking Ahead

After Tereshkova's landmark mission, it would take another 20 years for the United States to send a woman into space. Astronaut Sally Ride became the first female American astronaut to leave Earth on June 18, 1983. Since then, a total of 57 women from nine different countries have blasted off.

Two women are currently in orbit. NASA astronaut Karen Nyberg is aboard the International Space Station. Last week, China sent its second-ever female astronaut, Wang Yaping, to work on its orbiting space module. However, Tereshkova remains the only woman to complete a solo flight.

In recent years, NASA has run into trouble with funding. Currently, there are no American spacecraft that can carry humans to space. However, this new class of astronaut candidates suggests that NASA is looking ahead to the future of space exploration. The group includes the first female fighter pilot to become an astronaut in almost two decades, as well as a female helicopter pilot.

The class will begin training in August. "They're excited about the science we're doing on the International Space Station and our plan to . . . [go] there on spacecraft built by American companies," said NASA Administrator Charles Bolden in a statement. "And they're ready to help lead the first human mission to an asteroid and then on to Mars."

Considering the complexity. Having read the article ahead of time to consider what makes it complex, the teacher we were working with decided that the chronology of the article was one of the things that contributed to its complexity. Students reading the entire article would have to consider different years (1963, 1983, and the present) and what took place in each of them. In addition, the text is somewhat contradictory, in that while the article touts the achievements of women in space, the third paragraph lets readers know that NASA is no longer sending astronauts into space.

Here's how the teacher's interactions with one of her students played out while reading this text during guided reading:

The student reads the final two paragraphs aloud to the teacher. Her reading is relatively fluent, though she reads some of the second paragraph somewhat haltingly.

TEACHER: You read that well. I wonder if you can tell me, in general, the big ideas from this article. Think about what you read before as well as what you just read for me.

STUDENT: Well, it's about women who go into space.

TEACHER: Can you be more specific? Feel free to look back into the article.

STUDENT (looks down, doing some rereading to herself): I think the most important idea is that there are more female astronauts than ever before, and not just in the U.S., but in other countries, too.

TEACHER: Okay. So, what you just read interests me. I'd like you to consider how being a NASA astronaut today may be different from the way it was when Sally Ride went into space in 1983.

STUDENT: Well, I'd guess the technology is much better.

TEACHER: Does it say anything about the technology here? I want you to be paying attention to the text, okay?

STUDENT (looks down at text again): No, it doesn't . . . well, it's interesting because it says right here that NASA is not even sending astronauts into space right now because it costs too much.

TEACHER: Yes, I think that's interesting, too. How does that change your understanding of what you've read?

STUDENT: Um . . . (looks up at teacher and shrugs shoulders)

TEACHER: One of the things I want you to be thinking as you read articles like these is, "How does the information I'm reading in different paragraphs work together?" Sometimes authors will throw in information that is contradictory or that seems different from the rest. I want you to pay attention when that happens, and think about how that information may change your understanding of an article or passage. In this case, I was reading along and was very happy to see that there were more women in space programs than before, and then I got to this paragraph about how NASA isn't funding space travel now, and it made me think maybe the good news about women astronauts has to be taken with a grain of salt, because the space program in this country is quite different from what it was 30 or 50 years ago.

Notice how the teacher attempts to stretch her student's thinking about this passage. This conference reflects the teacher's efforts to get the student to think critically about text, placing it at Level 5 (critical understanding) on our continuum. The teacher recognized that, while much of the article is a relatively straightforward celebration of women's accomplishments as astronauts over the past 50 years, some information could be seen as tempering the celebration, and she wants the student to see that. There are other questions the teacher could have asked that would have also gotten this student to think critically, such as, "Why do you think that only one woman, a Russian, ever had a solo flight in space, and that was 50 years ago?" Generally, there is more than one right way to approach a text. What is notable is that the teacher asks a question that pushes beyond exclusively literal understanding of the text. The student doesn't answer the question this time, but the teacher provides her with sage advice for reading articles such as these, and over time, we would expect this student to pay attention to discrepant or unusual information within a text and do her best to make sense of it.

7TH-GRADE GUIDED READING GROUP

Note that although the following interaction took place in 7th grade, it took place with the teacher's struggling readers, and the text is written below the 7th-grade level. We actually encouraged the teacher to use this text, so that students in her group would not face decoding challenges that might relegate the teacher's work to Level 1 or Level 2 demands.

Text used: A portion of an article titled "Sorry Pilgrims, Christmas Shopping Season Just Started a Day Earlier" from newsela.com, November 17, 2013

Black Friday Becomes Black Thursday

The holiday shopping season used to start the day after Thanksgiving. The day became known as Black Friday. Now Black Friday may be dead. The family Thanksgiving dinner may be hurt, too.

Kmart might be the best example. It has been open for some hours on Thanksgiving for many years. But Kmart will open its doors at 6 a.m. on Thanksgiving. It will stay open for 41 hours. Macy's has been closed on Thanksgiving for 155 years. That streak will end this year. Macy's will open at 8 p.m. on Thanksgiving.

So will Sears. It will then stay open through the night. Sears will not close until 10 p.m. Friday. Wal-Mart, Target, Best Buy and many others will also have Thanksgiving hours.

"Thanksgiving used to be the one day retailers took a breather," said Bill Martin. He is the founder of ShopperTrak. His company gives advice to stores, or retailers. "Now that has changed. They're trying to get to the consumer's wallet as early as possible."

Stores have been racing to start the holiday season earlier. Now Black Friday is Black Thursday.

Why? There could be many reasons. There are not as many days between Thanksgiving and Christmas this year as there were last year. Hanukkah also comes very early. Stores may be scared of losing sales to a competitor. Shoppers also can just shop on an iPad at home whenever they want.

Considering the complexity. The teacher we worked with thought that background knowledge might add to the complexity of this article. She doesn't think most of her students' parents work in retail jobs, so they may not understand the implications of the article. In addition, the students' experience with Black Friday may be the news images one sees every Thanksgiving, of people pushing one another to get to particular items, and the violence that ensues. Bearing that in mind, the teacher approaches her work during guided reading in a very specific way.

The student reads a portion of this text aloud for the teacher, stumbling on a few words, including *Hanukkah* and *competitor*.

TEACHER: Jack, you read this really well. I know you didn't recognize every word here, but that matters less to me right now than whether or not you understood what you read. Do me a favor, and talk me through what you've read so far. What is going on in this article?

STUDENT: So, this article is about Black Friday, which is when people go shopping right after Thanksgiving.

TEACHER: Okay, that's true. Tell me more. Feel free to take a look at the article while you talk me through what is happening.

STUDENT (points to a heading): Well, it says that Black Friday is being moved to Thursday. Which is Thanksgiving. And it says that Thanksgiving dinner is being hurt.

TEACHER: Why is that?

STUDENT: Well, because more people could get hurt pushing each other when they're shopping on Thanksgiving?

TEACHER: Does it say that here? Please read back through this section more carefully, and when you're done, let me know why you think Thanksgiving dinner is being hurt.

STUDENT (spends a minute or two rereading silently): It doesn't say anything about people getting hurt, so I'm not sure why this hurts Thanksgiving dinner.

TEACHER: I want you to think about this, because as you get older, the articles you read may challenge you more. They won't always provide all the information you might need. Remember during shared reading, when I was thinking aloud about the polar ice caps article? There were a couple of spots where I couldn't figure out exactly what the author meant. Sometimes you have to be thoughtful and read between the lines. Go back and reread this section, and think the whole time about how moving the biggest shopping day of the year to Thanksgiving Day might impact Thanksgiving dinners.

In debriefing with this teacher after her guided reading lesson, we learned that she was surprised by how little her student appeared to understand about the article. She was concerned that this interaction was a failure. To the contrary, we believe that it was quite a successful interaction. Though the student may not really understand all the intricacies of the article, the teacher did three things that we believe will ultimately improve his competence in deriving meaning from texts. First of all, she determined that he had prior knowledge that was muddying his understanding, and she prompted him to make sure he was finding evidence within the text to support his thoughts. Second, she reminded him of the strategy the class worked on during shared reading. Finally, she gave him a clear purpose for reading through the article again, and let him know that the article may not spell out all the information he needs explicitly. Was the teacher confident that he'll be able to resolve his confusion? No. But the student does know that he didn't read carefully enough and that making meaning requires more than just a surface reading. During this interaction, the teacher asked the student to talk her through the article to demonstrate his understanding (Level 4, cumulative comprehension), and she also asked him to consider the implications of what he read (Level 5, critical understanding).

8TH-GRADE GUIDED READING GROUP

In this scenario, the 8th-grade language arts teacher works with his strongest readers. At our suggestion, he pulled an op-ed piece from the *New York Times*, hoping to find something that would challenge his students in a way that his publisher-provided leveled text sets had ceased to do.

Text used: An excerpt from a February 13, 2013, article by Gail Collins entitled "The State of the 4-Year-Olds"

One of the big moments of the State of the Union address was President Obama's call for "high-quality preschool" for 4-year-olds.

Nobody was happier at the idea than Walter Mondale, the former vice president. "This is going to be wonderful," he said in a phone conversation. His delight was sort of inspiring. If I had been down the road Mondale has traveled, my mood would have been a little darker.

In 1971, when he was a senator, Mondale led the Congressional drive to make quality preschool education available to every family in the United States that wanted it. *Everybody.* The federal government would set standards and provide backup services like meals and medical and dental checkups. Tuition would depend on the family's ability to pay.

And it passed! Then Richard Nixon vetoed it, claiming Congress was proposing "communal approaches to child rearing." Now, 42 years later, working parents of every economic level scramble madly to find quality programs for their preschoolers, while the waiting lines for poor families looking for subsidized programs stretch on into infinity.

And President Obama is trying, against great odds, to do something for 4-year-olds.

Considering the complexity. The teacher thought that this text would be challenging to his group because of the historical understanding (Who is Mondale? Who is Nixon?) as well as the structural knowledge of the federal government (understanding terms like *Congress, senator, veto,* and how they all fit together) that would be required to make sense of this text. In addition, he thought that the comparison between what happened in 1971 and what was happening in 2013 might be a challenge. With that in mind, he listened to the first student read the second and third paragraphs aloud. As expected, the student had no trouble reading the words of those paragraphs, nor did he pause or do anything that might pinpoint that comprehension had broken down.

TEACHER: You read that well. Why do you think the writer is writing about something that happened in 1971 when this article is supposed to be about Obama's push for high-quality pre-school for all students?

STUDENT: Well, it seems like this Mondale guy pushed for something similar back in 1971.

TEACHER: Why is it relevant to mention that here?

STUDENT (reads back through the passage): Because, really, if this Mondale guy's program had started, we'd already have high-quality preschool for every kid.

TEACHER: That's true. Think about what you know about politics now and think about what you just read. Do you notice any similarities?

STUDENT: Well . . . I hear a lot of people say that our government can't seem to get anything done. And it seems like back then, the same thing was true. Nixon, I think he was president, right? Well, he vetoed this, even though so many people supported it.

TEACHER: Yes. As you keep reading, I want you to continue thinking about the similarities and differences between our governments now and then.

Using opinion pieces like the one this teacher used often provides students the opportunity to "discern greater meaning," which is Level 6 of the Continuum of Task Complexity, because this kind of writing is designed to get readers thinking about how events and people fit together in the world. It also forces students to consider point of view, and how it may color a writer's perceptions of events. Consider another way this teacher could have approached his interaction with this student.

TEACHER: How do you think this author feels about the idea of preschool for every child?

STUDENT: It seems like she is for it.

TEACHER: How do you know? Look back at the article and see if you can point to something that makes you say that.

STUDENT: Well, in this paragraph, she describes what the program would have been like and how anybody who wanted it could get it. It seems very positive. And down here, she describes what's going on now, and she talks about how poor families are lined up into infinity to find good preschool for their kids. That seems negative. I think she would have preferred it to work out back in 1971.

TEACHER: Good, I think you're right. See if you can find more evidence as you read that supports your thinking about that.

This kind of interaction demonstrates Level 5 of the continuum, in that the student is asked to take the information given in the article and infer the writer's perspective. Note that while we distinguish between Level 5 and Level 6 interactions, both force students to push their thinking about text. This kind of conferencing with students is not second nature to most teachers; still, we encourage teachers to give it a try, knowing that there may be days, as there have been for some of the teachers in our examples, when their interactions fall short of their expectations. These important interactions get easier with time and practice, and the challenge of getting students to think deeply about the texts means that guided reading never becomes routine or boring. Every day is different, and every day brings new challenges.

CHAPTER 10

Epilogue:
On Shifts and Teacher Learning

Significant changes in pedagogical practice require a series of stops and starts. Often people must do something poorly before they do it well. The challenge in helping teachers implement the ideas in this book has been in their understandable reluctance to change comfortable practice in order to embark on the unknown. We get it. We also see how the new standards for reading, which call for greater emphasis on reading complex texts closely and with deep understanding, and the new standards for writing, which emphasize writing across genres, for multiple purposes and audiences, can seem overwhelming to teachers, particularly in the speed with which teachers are being asked to implement them. In this chapter, we share some of our own changes in thinking about reading and writing instruction, as we make the argument that teachers require time and practice to make reasonable and appropriate shifts in their instruction.

Our own journey toward greater understanding of the ways children gain sophistication in their reading and writing has involved our own sputters. Initially, we believed that writing conferences could contain both lower- and higher-level concerns. We worked with teachers to help them give multiple layers of feedback in a single sitting with a student. We have since discovered that the practice of mixing feedback levels resulted in the student becoming much more engaged with the simpler task and leaving the more complicated one unattended. Based upon those observations, we removed that portion from our model of writing conferences. Since we understand the importance of this kind of feedback, we designed whole-group minilessons that addressed the simpler writing processes that could be reasonably taught to the whole group. In our current thinking, we want the teacher to use the valuable time working with an individual student only on less discrete concerns, feedback that is not easily used to improve a single paper and then forgotten. We know that we have gained singular attention to a sophisticated task, and we know that we have given up, perhaps, an easy improvement to a given paper. Looking back at our previous work, we note suggestions that we no longer would make. Our shift in thinking dovetails with the new standards for writing, which place significant emphasis on higher-level writing skills such as "conveying complex ideas," "analyzing substantive topics," and clearly understanding "task, purpose, and audience."

Our previous books on guided reading encourage teachers to be as "in the moment" with the student reader as possible in that teachers could not predict the kinds of questions they might ask. We were eager for teachers to implement small-group reading instruction, and were wary of asking them to plan for multiple groups. Indeed, one of our fundamental principles for responsive guided reading was that it required minimal planning. While we still discourage teachers from planning before or after reading discussion questions, vocabulary study, or strategy lessons, we now see that the kinds of conversations we hope teachers will have with students do require a good understanding of the text and a notion of what will make a particular text difficult for a student. While this may not feel like planning in the traditional sense, we want to be clear that we now believe that teachers will need to put time into preparing the text. Our preparation includes doing a close reading prior to introducing the text to students. Additionally, we try to orient ourselves to the complexity of the particular text so that we are prepared for how that complexity might affect a student reader. Many teachers will find themselves selecting texts for students that are out of their own interest, on unfamiliar topics or, in the case of strong middle grade readers, just plain hard. Even upper elementary informational texts can require our entire arsenal of strategies so that we are able to make meaning of them at the most sophisticated level. In our previous books, we advertised these groups as involving little planning, and we now think of that element differently. While we aren't planning for instruction the way we do in some other areas of literacy education, with objectives, outcomes, and assessments predetermined, we are thinking through what the objectives and outcomes of a particular text might be and how to determine student facility with it. Again, this shift in our thinking mirrors the demands of the new standards in reading that ask students to "make logical inferences" using "textual evidence . . . to support conclusions," "analyze the structure of texts," "evaluate the argument and specific claims in a text," and so on. Clearly, we need to elevate the substance of our individual interactions with students so that students begin to see reading as much more than accuracy, fluency, and answering simple questions. As Pearson (2013) suggests, teacher scaffolding of student reading is absolutely necessary in order to support students in meeting these expectations.

These are just two of the adjustments we have made to our thinking as we have worked with students and teachers. We look back with mixed feelings on our previous work. On the one hand, we are sorry not to have given every teacher the benefit of everything we now know. On the other, though, our work with those teachers is what has prompted the evolution of our ideas. We know that teachers who try out these practices will stumble and adjust as we did. We also know that they may regret not helping every single student in the most effective way possible, but that is life in schools. Knowledge changes, teachers change, student needs change. We do what we can with what we know when we know it.

In the midst of change, it is ever so tempting to revert back to the practice to which we were accustomed. This is chronic in the world of instructional change in schools. Administrators and teachers themselves often aren't patient enough to let teacher learning grow. When teachers don't feel confident with new practices, they panic and default back to the comfortable. When they aren't very good when they start, they see it as an indictment of the practice or their own abilities.

Teachers must see themselves as the unit of change before they can examine any change that might occur in student learning. They have to worry about their own learning, let their own knowledge grow, practice new instruction, talk with colleagues and supervisors, read, and think. Unfortunately, the pace of school is such that these processes are rarely valued. This book takes as central that the reading and writing conferences that we describe are focused upon teaching about reading and writing themselves more than teaching reading and writing about any particular text. To do so, teachers will have to think of the big picture in student learning and use the opportunities they have to interact with students around their reading and writing as part of a year-long conversation about literacy. It is the same with teacher learning about these kinds of practices. For the 1st year, teachers will need to use the opportunities to work with students in this way as examinations of their own teaching. Sometimes the interactions will feel successful. Other times the interactions will be deeply dissatisfying, and teachers will have to trust that continued work of this kind will yield growth in student literacy. It is a lot for us to ask teachers to grant our work that trust.

When we work with schools and districts, we alert the administration that the implementation of this kind of reading and writing instruction takes time. We share that the 1st year should be focused on teachers and their own learning about these practices, about what it means to look at complex texts with their students. If they aren't permitted this year of growth, they will likely never feel competent and often revert back to old ways that aren't as complex for certain, but also don't yield the richness that conferences of this sort really do.

We also insist that administrators know that teachers cannot make deep changes to practice in isolation. Collaboration with peers is probably the most important element, and principals who encourage this kind of work are convinced of its value as are we. Beyond just grade-level meetings, though, we have seen the power of peer observation even when both teachers are at the learning stage. In the busyness of the school day, these kinds of interactions, focused peer visits, can get pushed off the to-do list, but we believe in their value and note that they can often be accomplished without a lot of jostling of schedules while one or another teacher is relieved of their class by the physical education or art teacher or as their students visit the library or the playing field during recess.

We tell students that learning is a risk, that complex processes like reading and writing take time and much practice, that intellectual growth is not linear or predictable. It is the same with teaching. Change over time requires courage, support, and trust. We hope to continue this dialogue as teachers and students begin the kinds of interactions that we believe will push them momentarily out of their comfort zone, into teaching and learning that continually challenges but also engages in meaningful ways.

We leave you with a few suggestions for getting started:

1. Make time to meet with individual students about their reading and writing as soon as possible. Don't worry if you are not able to meet with every student as expeditiously as you might like. Just give it a try. While students are writing, pull a student or two and ask them to read you what they've been writing. If you don't already do guided reading, set a goal to meet with two groups per week, for just 20 minutes. As you get used to this kind of work, try to meet with more students.

2. Make a copy of the Continuums for Task Complexity During Writing Conferences and Guided Reading, and bring those with you to your individual interactions. Challenge yourself to ignore the lower-level needs of your students and try out the tasks on the right side of the continuum. Be sure to let your students know that this is something you're working on to better support them as readers and writers.

3. Use more informational texts. Create a folder of nonfiction articles (see our list of potential resources in Chapter 8) and use them during guided reading. Worry less about precise reading level and more about providing students with interesting but challenging texts that require teacher support for making meaning. These texts will not be the same for all students, so make sure you find texts that provide a range of challenges. Share resources with your grade-level colleagues as well as across grade levels.

4. Give students as much latitude in selecting their own writing topics as possible. Embrace the idea that the word *author* is related to the word *authority*, that most great writing comes from interest, passion, and knowledge, and that these come from student agency.

5. Give yourself time to become proficient at this work. Know that change doesn't happen instantly. Work with your colleagues and share your starts and stops, so that you feel sup-

ported. Invite a colleague or two into your classroom to observe your individual interactions with students to get their feedback. Observe your colleagues as well.

We look forward to a dialogue with our readers. Please contact us as you try out these ideas and come up with modifications that might help us.

References

Albright, L. K., & Ariail, M. (2005). Tapping the potential of teacher read-alouds in middle schools. *Journal of Adolescent & Adult Literacy, 48*(7), 582–591.

Allington, R. L., & Johnston, P. H. (2002). *Reading to learn: Lessons from exemplary 4th grade classrooms.* New York: Guilford.

Anderson, L. M., Evertson, C. M., & Brophy, J. E. (1979). An experimental study of effective teaching in first-grade reading groups. *The Elementary School Journal, 79*(4), 193–223.

Anderson, R. C., Wilkinson, I. A. G., & Mason, J. M. (1991). A microanalysis of the small-group, guided reading lesson: Effects of an emphasis on global story meaning. *Reading Research Quarterly, 26*(4), 417–441.

Anderson, T., O'Leary, D., Schuler, K., & Wright, L. (2002). *Increasing reading comprehension through the use of guided reading.* Master of Arts Action Research Project, Saint Xavier University.

Argyle, M. (1976). Personality and social behavior. In R. Harre (Ed.), *Personality*, (pp. 145–188). Oxford, UK: Blackwell.

Atwell, N. (2014). *In the middle: A lifetime of learning about writing, reading, and adolescents* (3rd ed.). Portsmouth, NH: Heinemann.

Bayraktar, A. (2013). Nature of interactions during teacher-student writing conferences, revisiting the potential effects of self-efficacy beliefs. *Egitim Arastirmalari-Eurasian Journal of Educational Research, 50,* 63–86.

Bear, D., Invernizzi, M., Templeton, S., & Johnston, F. (2011). *Words their way: Word study for phonics, vocabulary and spelling instruction* (5th ed.). New York, NY: Pearson.

Beers, K., & Probst, R. E. (2012). *Notice and note: Strategies for close reading.* Portsmouth, NH: Heinemann.

Bell, M. A. (2002). Teacher feature: Why use an interactive whiteboard? A baker's dozen reasons! *Teachers.net Gazette, 3*(1).

Berne, J. I. (2008). *The writing-centered classroom: Writing workshop in the high school.* New York, NY: Guilford Press.

Berne, J. I., & Degener, S. D. (2010). *Responsive guided reading.* New York, NY: Guilford Press.

Berne, J. I., & Degener, S. D. (2012). *Strategic reading instruction: Guiding middle grade readers.* Thousand Oaks, CA: Corwin Press.

Blachowicz, C. L. Z., Fisher, P. J. L., & Ogle, D. (2006). Vocabulary: Questions from the classroom. *Reading Research Quarterly, 41*(4), 524–539.

Blachowicz, C. L. Z., Obrochta, C., & Fogelberg, E. (2005). Literacy coaching for change. *Educational Leadership, March,* 55–58.

Black, L. J. (1998). Between talk and teaching: Reconsidering the writing conference. *All USU Press Publications,* Book 121.

Block, C. C. (1993). Strategy instruction in a literature-based reading program. *The Elementary School Journal, 94*(2), 139–151.

Block, C. C., & Pressley, M. (2002). *Comprehension instruction: Research-based best practices.* New York, NY: Guilford Press.

Boreen, J. (1995). *The language of reading conferences.* Annual meeting of the National Council of Teachers of English. San Diego, California.

Boushey, G., & Moser, J. (2009). The *CAFÉ book.* Portland, ME: Stenhouse.

Boushey, G., & Moser, J. (2014). *The daily five: Fostering literacy independence in the elementary grades* (2nd ed.). Portland, ME: Stenhouse.

Brown, S. (2013). An analysis of the discourse and actions of reading conferences with English learners: A situated perspective. *Literacy Research and Instruction, 52*(2), 130–149.

Calkins, L. M. (1980). When children want to punctuate: Basic skills belong in context. *Language Arts, 57*(5), 567–573.

Calkins, L. M. (1994). *The art of teaching writing* (2nd ed.). Portsmouth, NH: Heinemann.

Calkins, L. M. (2003). *The nuts and bolts of teaching writing.* Portsmouth, NH: Heinemann.

Calkins, L.M. (2006). *A guide to the writing workshop, Grades 3–5.* Portsmouth, NH: Heinemann.

Cambourne, B. (1988). *The whole story: Natural learning and the acquisition of literacy in the classroom.* Auckland, New Zealand: Ashton Scholastic.

Collins, G. (2013, February 13). The state of the 4-year-olds. *The New York Times.* Retrieved from http://www.nytimes.com/2013/02/14/opinion/collins-the-state-of-the-4-year-olds.html?_r=0

Connor, M. C., Piasta, S. B., Fishman, B., Glasney, S., Schatschneider, C., Crowe, E., Underwood, P., & Morrison, F. J. (2009). Individualizing student instruction precisely: Effects of child by instruction interactions on first graders' literacy development. *Child Development, 80*(1), 77–100.

Cotton, K. (1998). *Education for lifelong learning: Literature synthesis.* Washington, DC: Office of Educational Research and Improvement (ERIC Document Reproduction Service No. ED 422 608).

Cramer, R. (2001). *Creative power: The nature and nurture of children's writing.* New York, NY: Longman.

Degener, S., & Berne, J. (n.d.). Unpublished raw data.

Dorn, L., & Jones, T. (2012). *Apprenticeship in literacy: Transitions across reading and writing, K–4* (2nd ed.). Portland, ME: Stenhouse.

Duke, N. K., & Pearson, P. (2002). Effective practices for developing reading comprehension. In A. E. Farstrup & S. Samuels (Eds.), *What research has to say about reading instruction* (3rd ed., pp. 205–242). Newark, DE: International Reading Association.

Elbow, P. (1973). *Writing without teachers.* New York, NY: Oxford University Press.

Elbow, P. (1981). *Writing with power.* New York, NY: Oxford University Press.

Fisher, D., Frey, N., & Lapp, D. (2011). *Teaching students to read like detectives: Comprehending, analyzing, and discussing texts.* Indiana University: Solution Tree Press.

Fletcher, R. (2013) *What a writer needs* (2nd ed.). Portsmouth, NH: Heinemann.

Fletcher, R., & Portalupi, J. (2001). *Writing workshop: The essential guide.* Portland, ME: Stenhouse.

Flower, L. (1987). Interpretive acts: Cognition and the construction of discourse. *Poetics, 16,* 109–130.

Flynn, T., & King, M. (1993). *Dynamics of the writing conference: Social and cognitive interaction.* Urbana, IL: National Council of Teachers of English.

García, G. E., Pearson, P. D., Taylor, B. M., Bauer, E. B., & Stahl, K. A. D. (2011). Socio-constructivist and political views on teachers' implementation of two types of reading comprehension approaches in low-income schools. *Theory into Practice, 50*(2), 149–156.

Gill, S. R. (2000). Reading with Amy: Teaching and learning through reading conferences. *The Reading Teacher, 53*(6), 500–509.

Graham, S., & Perin, D. (2006). *Writing next: Effective strategies to improve writing of adolescents in middle and high schools.* A report to the Carnegie Corporation of New York: Washington, DC: Alliance for Excellent Education.

Graves, D. (1983). *Writing: Teachers and children at work.* Portsmouth, NH: Heinemann.

Graves, D. (1994). *A fresh look at writing.* Portsmouth, NH: Heinemann.

Haneda, M. (2004). The joint construction of meaning in writing conference. *Applied Linguistics, 25*(2), 178–219.

Harris, M. (1995). Talking in the middle: Why writers need writing tutors. *College English, 57*(1), 27–42.

Heath, S. B. (2012). *Words at work and play: Three decades in family and community life.* Cambridge, UK: Cambridge University Press.

Ivey, G., & Baker, M. I. (2004). Phonics instruction for older students? Just say no. *Educational Leadership, 61*(6), 35–39.

Ivey, G., & Broaddus, K. (2001). "Just plain reading": A survey of what makes students want to read in middle school classrooms. *Reading Research Quarterly, 36*(4), 350–377.

Jacobs, V. A. (2002). Reading, writing, and understanding. *Educational Leadership, 60*(3), 58–61.

Lenz, B. K., Ehren, B. J., & Deshler, D. D. (2005). The content literacy continuum: A school reform framework for improving adolescent literacy for all students. *Teaching Exceptional Children, 37*(6), 60–63.

McCarthey, S. J. (1992). The teacher, the author, and the text: Variations in form and content of writing conferences. *Journal of Literacy Research, 24*(1), 51–82.

McIver, M. C., & Wolf, S. A. (1998). *Writing conferences: Powerful tools for writing instruction.* Lost Angeles, CA: National Center for Research on Evaluation, University of California, Los Angeles.

Moje, E. B. (1996). "I teach students, not subjects": Teacher-student relationships as contexts for secondary literacy. *Reading Research Quarterly*, *31*(2), 172–195.

Newkirk, T. (1995). The writing conference as performance. *Research in the Teaching of English*, *29*(2), 193–215.

Palinscar, A. S. (1984). The quest for meaning from expository text: A teacher guided journey. In G. Duffy, L. Roehler, & J. Mason (Eds.), *Comprehension instruction: Perspectives and suggestions*. New York, NY: Longman.

Parsons, S. A. (2012). Adaptive teaching in literacy instruction: Case studies of two teachers. *Journal of Literacy Research*, *44*(2), 149–170.

Pearson, P. D. (2013). Research foundations of the Common Core State Standards in English language arts. In S. B. Neumann & L. B. Gambrell (Eds.), *Quality reading instruction in the age of Common Core Standards* (pp. 237–262). Newark, DE: International Reading Association.

Raphael, T. E. (1982). Question-answering strategies for children. *Reading Teacher*, *37*, 186–191.

Raphael, T. E. (1986). Teaching question answer relationships, revisited. *Reading Teacher*, *39*, 516–522.

Raphael, T. E., & Au, K. H. (2005). QAR: Enhancing comprehension and test taking across grades and content areas. *The Reading Teacher*, *59*(3), 206–221.

Ray, K. W. (2004) *Writing workshop with our youngest writers*. Portsmouth, NH: Heinemann.

Ray, K. W., & Laminack, L. L. (2001). *The writing workshop. Working through the hard parts (and they're all hard parts)*. Urbana, IL: National Council of Teachers of English.

Rosenblatt, L. (1994). *The reader, the text, the poem: The transactional theory of the literary work*. Carbondale, IL: Southern Illinois University Press.

Routman, R. (2002). Teacher talk. *Educational Leadership*, *59*(6), 32–35.

Schoenbach, R., Greenleaf, C., & Murphy, L. (2012). *Reading for understanding: How reading apprenticeship improves disciplinary learning in secondary and college classrooms*. San Francisco, CA: Jossey-Bass.

Shanahan, T. (2012). The Common Core ate my baby and other urban legends. *Educational Leadership*, *70*(4), 10–16.

Smith, M. W., Cheville, J., & Hillocks, G. (2006). I guess I'd better watch my English: Grammars in the teaching of the English Language Arts. In C. A. MacArthur, S. Graham, & J. Fitzgerald (Eds.), *Handbook of Writing Research* (pp. 275–292). New York, NY: Guilford.

Sperling, M. (1991). Dialogues of deliberation: Conversation in the teacher-student writing conference. *Written Communication*, *8*(2), 131–162.

Stahl, S. A. (1998). Understanding shifts in reading and its instruction. *Peabody Journal of Education*, *73*(3–4), 31–67.

Taylor, B. M., Pearson, P. D., Clark, K., & Walpole, S. (2000). Effective schools and accomplished teachers: Lessons about primary-grade reading instruction in low-income schools. *Elementary School Journal*, *101*(2), 121–165.

VanDeWeghe, R. (2007). Writing policy and school reform. *English Journal*, 96(4), 94–98,

Vygotsky, L. (1978). *Mind and society*. Cambridge, MA: Harvard University Press.

Wilson-Powers, S. (1999). *The examination of teacher discourse with four Eastern Kentucky fourth-graders during writing conferences.* Unpublished doctoral dissertation, University of Kentucky.

Young, R., & Miller, E. (2004). Learning as changing participation: Discourse roles in ESL writing conferences. *Modern Language Journal, 88*, 519–535.

Index

About the Authors

Jennifer Berne is associate professor and department chair of Literacy Education and Elementary Education at Northern Illinois University. She can be contacted at Jberne@niu.edu.

Sophie Degener is associate professor of Reading and Language at National Louis University. She can be contacted at Sophie.Degener@nl.edu.